"Want to be forev⟨ ⟩ condemnation? *Grace for Disgrace* is a masterful, MUST READ for this generation.

Pastor Gary Hooper has packed into each page transforming revelation designed to set you free. Through this book, you will regain the joy and liberty of your salvation by understanding the grace of Jesus Christ. *Grace for Disgrace* will banish condemnation from your life once and for all and allow your faith to leap to miracle working levels!

This is the best book we have read in years! We are forever changed by the wisdom within these pages. Let that wisdom and understanding empower you, shape you, and set you apart for God's master plan."

— Len & Cathy Mink

"I have known Pastor Gary for most of my Christian life. Having been born again and raised up under Pastor Gary's tutelage, he has been and still is a mentor as well as a very close friend. I am proud to say that he is my spiritual father and I have had the honour of working alongside him in the ministry for over eighteen years now. If not for his selfless acts and bringing me in under his wing, I don't know where I'd be today. I've watched him go through some of the fiercest storms and through it all he still remains standing at his post and standing in faith believing God.

With his voracious hunger for the Word of God, I was not surprised when Pastor Gary decided to write his first book. He is a student of the Word, always studying to show himself approved and his wisdom and insight into God's Word always amazes me! *Grace for Disgrace* is a necessary teaching for today since many people have been living such defeated lives. This book will help us to live victoriously in these perilous times!"

— Pastor Paul C. Wilson

"Everybody needs to read this book. Gary has taken the revelation that God gave him and made it easy to understand. This holy information will raise the quality of your life. I love, respect and trust Gary Hooper for many reasons, but most of all because he practices what he preaches."

— Mylon LeFevre

GRACE
FOR
DISGRACE

From Religion To Reality

GARY HOOPER

GRACE FOR DISGRACE

Copyright © 2012 by Gary L. Hooper

All Scripture quotations, unless otherwise specified, are from The Holy Bible, King James Version. Copyright © 1977, 1984, Thomas Nelson Inc., Publishers. Scripture quotations marked "AMP" taken from the Amplified® Bible, Copyright © 1954, 1958, 1962, 1964, 1965, 1987 by The Lockman Foundation. Used by permission (www.lockman.org). Scriptures and additional materials quoted are from the Good News Bible © 1994 published by the Bible Societies/ HarperCollins Publishers Ltd UK, Good News Bible © American Bible Society 1966, 1971, 1976, 1992. Used with permission. Scripture quotations marked "CJB" are taken from the Complete Jewish Bible, copyright 1998 by David H. Stern. Published by Jewish New Testament Publications, Inc. (www. messianicjewish.net/jntp). Distributed by Messianic Jewish Resources Int'l (www.messianicjewish.net). All rights reserved. Used by permission.

ISBN:978-1-77069-456-9

Printed in Canada.

Word Alive Press
131 Cordite Road, Winnipeg, MB R3W 1S1
www.wordalivepress.ca

Library and Archives Canada Cataloguing in Publication

Hooper, Gary L., 1949-
    Grace for disgrace : from religion
to reality / Gary L. Hooper.

ISBN 978-1-77069-456-9

    1. Shame--Religious aspects--Christianity.
2. Christian life. I. Title.

BT714.H66 2012   233'.4   C2011-908445-7

d e d i c a t i o n

I dedicate this work to my wife Nancy and our children for all their love and support, and to the staff and congregation of New Covenant Church, as we work together with Jesus in promoting the Kingdom of God.

table of contents

acknowledgements

I want to thank the many gifted and dedicated teachers whose teachings have fuelled my quest to know God. Kenneth E. Hagin, Kenneth Copeland, Creflo Dollar, Jesse Duplantis, Bill Winston, George Moss, Mylon LeFevre, Len Mink, Dr. Dennis Burke, Mark Hankins, Lorne Rostotski and so many more. I learned much of grace many years ago from Bob Yandian and Tony Cooke.

I appreciate Beth MacDonald for all of her hard work and dedication to this project.

Most of all I want to thank the Holy Spirit of God for taking the things of Jesus and giving us the revelation within these pages.

A special thank you to Pastors Steve and Shirley Pardy, for showing me how to walk by faith.

introduction

Paul told Timothy that all Scripture is God-breathed and that it is for inspiration, edification, correction and instruction. We are to study in order to show ourselves approved, for you can't preach half the truth.

I want to show you in God's Word how the Old Testament is the New Testament concealed, and the New Testament is the Old Testament revealed. I once heard a preacher say that you can't preach out of the Old Testament, but if that's the case you shouldn't be preaching at all, because how do you separate it? I understand separating the law from grace, but you need to understand disgrace in order to walk in God's grace.

We've all experienced disgrace, and we all know what it feels like. We've experienced shame, but then we found out that Paul told Timothy that he wasn't ashamed. He had gotten to the place where he served God with a pure conscience, like his forefathers (2 Timothy 1:3). This is coming from a man who had murdered people in his past life, yet he could say that his conscience was pure. I know people who have been saved for twenty years who can't say that; they still feel guilt and shame. Paul the Apostle found a way to get past that shame and guilt, because he understood grace. He understood that when he wrote to the church at Ephesus and told them, "You are saved by grace, through faith and it's not of yourselves: it's a gift from God and it's not of works lest anyone should boast" (Ephesians 2:9, paraphrased).

When it comes to grace, there's nothing to brag about. There's nothing to brag about when it's a gift. Romans 5:17 says that those who receive the gift of righteousness will reign in life by Christ Jesus. So, when you recognize the fact that righteousness is a gift, you can flow in it. There is only one gift you need to unwrap in the Word of God—and it's grace. Grace brings ease for dis-ease. God's not mad at you, nor will He ever be mad at you. God loves you and His grace abounds towards you. He's just tickled over you, and I want to prove it to you in this teaching.

As you receive the revelation printed on these pages, I believe you will never be the same again! You will never have another guilty day. You will never again feel shame and you will never again feel condemnation. Fear will leave you, sickness won't be able to stay with you, and prosperity will seek you out! My prayer is that you won't receive information, but rather revelation. It's nice when you get some information, but revelation will far surpass it every time. You can know something intellectually, but when it goes off *inside of you*, that's revelation. When God showed me this revelation, it totally set me free. I don't think there is anyone this won't help.

Many people on earth, from all religions, aim to please God with their works, and much of the body of Christ tries to do the same thing. All the religions of the world are trying to reach God, but God reached down and touched mankind through His grace. When you try to please God through your works, what you are saying is that it wasn't enough for Jesus to die on the cross.

As we look into God's Word, we will see why some people get healed and some people don't. We will see why some people walk in prosperity and others do not. We will answer all those questions if you just receive the revelation and don't let it go. You need to feed this revelation into our spirit, because in it you will find total freedom and liberty.

You can be carefree!

NO CONDEMNATION

chapter one

SELF-RIGHTEOUSNESS VS. RIGHTEOUSNESS BY FAITH

In John 21, Jesus reaches out to Peter because Peter was feeling condemned, guilty, and full of shame. Even though he knew he was called to be a fisher of men, he thought that surely he couldn't be one anymore, not after what he had done, having denied the Lord three times, shamed himself by cursing in front of a young woman, and totally messed up his testimony. Through this, we see how Jesus prepared a meal for him, and how Peter couldn't wait for the boat to get ashore. In fact, he swam ashore to get there faster.

Jesus began to talk to Peter in John 21:15–17. Peter had denied Him three times, and in these verses Jesus asked Peter three times, "Do you love me?" Each time, Peter had to confess, "I don't *agape* love you, Jesus. You know that. I don't sacrificially love you. I *phileo* love you, I love you like a brother." That's why Peter believed he had failed Jesus.

Jesus said to him, "Peter, Satan has desired to sift all of you disciples like wheat. I prayed for you, that your faith wouldn't fail." Peter stood up and said, "Lord, I am ready to go with you both to prison and death" (Luke 22:33, paraphrased). His dependence on himself is really self-righteousness.

Whenever you say, "I'm convinced that I can do this. Today, I'm going to get it right. Yesterday I screwed it up, but today I know I'm going to get it right. I'm determined." Anytime you are dependent on yourself, it is not good.

Jesus says to Peter, "If you love me, you get to feed my sheep. I'm inviting you back to the call that I put on your life initially. Peter, you are not condemned. You are going to go preach, and what you are going to preach is grace."

NO CONDEMNATION

In John 8, a woman caught in adultery is brought before Jesus. The scribes and Pharisees are trying to trap Him with their religion. John 8:2–3 says,

> *And early in the morning he came again into the temple, and all the people came unto him; and he sat down, and taught them. And the scribes and Pharisees brought unto him a woman taken in adultery; and when they had set her in the midst...*

They basically threw her in the middle of the crowd. Can you imagine the shame of that? Can you imagine the condemnation this woman was experiencing? There she was, being treated like garbage and thrown into the middle of the crowd.

> *They say unto him, Master, this woman was taken in adultery, in the very act. Now Moses in the law commanded us, that such should be stoned: but what sayest thou? [What do you say, Jesus?] This they said, tempting him, that they might have to accuse him. But Jesus stooped down, and with his finger wrote on the ground, as though he heard them not. (John 8:4–6)*

We need to know what He wrote in the ground. There have been many teachings about how it was the religious leaders' girlfriends' names, but in Jeremiah 17:13 we see what he wrote:

Oh Lord, the hope of Israel, all that forsake thee shall be ashamed, and they that depart from me shall be written in the earth [in the dirt], because they have forsaken the Lord, the fountain of living waters.

He had just finished saying, *"I am the living water."* And instead the religious leaders went out and found a woman in adultery and threw her down, so He simply got down and began to write their own names in the dirt. They would understand the significance of this, because they'd had to memorize Scripture. They would have remembered Jeremiah 17:13 and known what He was talking about when He wrote in the dirt, which is why they quietly left.

So when they continued asking him, he lifted up himself, and said unto them, He that is without sin among you, let him first cast a stone at her. And again he stooped down, and wrote on the ground. And they which heard it, being convicted by their own conscience, went out one by one, beginning at the eldest, even unto the last: and Jesus was left alone, and the woman standing in the midst. When Jesus had lifted up himself, and saw none but the woman, he said unto her, Woman, where are those thine accusers? hath no man condemned thee? She said, No man, Lord. [The message that He brought to this woman comes next.] And Jesus said unto her, Neither do I condemn thee: go, and sin no more. (John 8:7–11)

You need to underline that part in your Bible. Most people would emphasize *"Go, and sin no more,"* which is an absolute impossibility. What Jesus is really saying is, "I'm releasing you from condemnation."

When you get released from condemnation, sin won't be a problem anymore, because suddenly you're not going to be dependent on yourself. You see, the strength of sin is condemnation. The strength of sin, as the

Bible says in 1 Corinthians 15, is the law. So if there is no condemnation, sin loses its strength. What He's saying to her is this: "I have something for you—the gift of grace." In other words, He has grace for us!

REDEEMED FROM THE CURSE OF THE LAW

Galatians 3:13 tells us that we've been redeemed from something. What have we been redeemed from? The answer is the curse of the law, but what is the curse of the law? I once would have said sin and death, sickness and poverty—but sin, death, sickness, and poverty are only the *results* of the curse. The curse is condemnation.

How do we know that? Adam, in Genesis 3:10, said that he hid because he was afraid. In other words, he felt condemned, so when he heard God's voice, he went the other way.

This example shows us that condemnation came before sin, death, poverty, or sickness ever came to Adam. The condemnation had to come first, because without condemnation sin has no power, sickness has no power, and poverty has no power. The only power any of these things have is condemnation. If you don't have it, the curse can't touch you. So, the first thing that the curse brings is condemnation. The moment that I accept guilt, the moment that I accept shame, the moment that I accept condemnation, I am under the law and I am self-righteous.

Paul taught this in the book of Romans. When God gave me this revelation, everything just fell together. It was like the first sixteen chapters of Romans just all fell over like dominoes, one after the other. I saw the whole thing encapsulated and thought, *That's right! Just believing that I can keep the law exposes me to sin.*

Let's back up to Galatians 3:10, where it says, *"For as many as are of the works of the law are under the curse."* So, what Paul's saying is that I'm put under the curse just by believing I can keep the law. Relying on oneself is really what self-righteousness is.

During a recent visit to Israel, while up on the Temple Mount, I realized that every religion of the world was there and they were all trying to reach God, trying to please Him with their rituals and human effort. As I watched, God showed me that it's the same in the church. We are saved by grace, through faith, and we didn't do it on our own. It is a gift from God, not of our own works. And yet many in the church are still working, trying to please God.

As long as we are *doing*, we don't accept the fact that it is *done*. Because once it's done, Hebrews 4:11 says that we should labour to enter into His rest. You see, there is a place of rest in God, and in that place it's possible for us to rest in what has already been done, not in what we are doing. You and I need to have more faith in what He has done than what we're doing at any given time.

Romans 10:3 says, about the Hebrew people, *"For they [were] being ignorant of God's righteousness [which is by faith], and going [went] about to establish their own righteousness…"*

To our modern thinking, we would think, *Wow, that's so dumb.* When I was in Israel, I saw how dumb religion is, and then I got back home and I saw how dumb *mine* is. Religion is inside us every single day and we can suddenly slip over into it, without even realizing, because we've been brought up to be performance-oriented. We think to ourselves, *I've got to perform. If I can just get these things done right, surely God will be pleased.*

No. As a matter of fact, the opposite is true.

For as many as are of the works of the law are under the curse: for it is written, Cursed is every one that continueth not in all things which are written in the book of the law to do them. (Galatians 3:10)

So, how do I know I'm right? Have you ever done something and felt like kicking yourself? That's the law! Have you ever said, "I have to get this right, I have to do better tomorrow, and I'm tired of failing in this area"? That's self-righteous, because you're still saying that *I* have to get this right and *I* have got to be a better Christian. How can *I* be a Christian and act that way? No. *You* can't do this. *You* can't do one thing. He already did it all for you, so you wouldn't have to do a thing.

One thing that gets me about the Word is that Jesus said, *"As ye have therefore received [learned] Christ Jesus the Lord, so walk ye in him"* (Colossians 2:6). I learned about Him in a drug dependency centre where I could do nothing to help myself. Then, when I got some Christianity under my belt, I thought, *I'm going to do this.* No. The verse says that as you receive Him, continue in that. Continue being totally dependent upon Him. That's it! We don't have to depend on ourselves. We depended on ourselves before we got saved and that certainly didn't work out well for us then, so why do we think we can do any better now?

A NEW CALENDAR

To further understand our redemption we need to go back to the book of Genesis.

Genesis 8:1–4 says,

> *And God remembered Noah, and every living thing, and all the cattle that was with him in the ark: and God made a wind to pass over the earth, and the waters assuaged [stopped]; the fountains of the deep and the windows of heaven were stopped, and the rain from heaven was restrained; and the waters returned from off the earth continually: and after the end of the hundred and fifty days the waters were abated. And the ark rested in the seventh month, on the seventeenth day of the month, upon the mountains of Ararat.*

The seventeenth day of the seventh month, on the calendar they were operating on in the book of Genesis, would have been Passover. The seventeenth of the month, in fact, would have been equivalent to the Sunday when Jesus rose from the grave. This seventh month became the first month in Exodus 12, when God gave the wandering Israelites a new calendar. He said, "Not only are you free from slavery, but this will be the first day, the first month for you." In other words, "This is your calendar, and it's not an Egyptian calendar. This is going to be the first day of the month for you, the beginning of months."

He gave them this calendar, and when they left Egypt they passed over the Red Sea and came up on the other side on Nisan 17, the same day as when Noah's ark touched ground after its long voyage. Then, when Joshua, Aaron, and the children of Israel crossed over the Jordan

River, they came up against Jericho—once again, on the same day. Nisan 17 was also when Jesus rose from the grave.

So, Nisan 17 is when the ark landed on the Mountains of Ararat. This is not just the name of a mountain in Turkey; "Arar" means curse, and when you put the "at" on the end, it means the curse reversed. So, even in the beginning, God showed His grace.

THE RAVEN—UNCLEAN

It says in Genesis 8:5–7,

And the waters decreased continually until the tenth month: in the tenth month, on the first day of the month, were the tops of the mountains seen. And it came to pass at the end of forty days, that Noah opened the window of the ark which he had made: and he sent forth a raven [an unclean bird], which went forth to and fro, until the waters were dried up from off the earth.

The expression "to and fro" is seen again later in the Bible. In Job 1, when God asks Satan where he has been, Satan answered, "I've been going to and fro throughout the earth." You see, the raven represents a type of the devil. The raven went out and didn't have to come back because it was busy feeding—on floating corpses. The earth was cursed, so the raven could only land on the things that were condemned. Put another way, we could say that the raven could only land on things that were under condemnation. The raven could only feed on flesh, therefore if you are in the flesh the raven can feed on you. The raven was living on something that was condemned, which is the only thing it can live on today.

THE DOVE—CLEAN

God recently gave me a great revelation about the dove. I used to ask, "God, why would You use the dove as a symbol of the Holy Spirit when I know the Holy Spirit isn't a bird?" We read in Luke 3 that He descended in bodily form like a dove and now, I understand why he sent out the dove. The dove cannot rest on anything unclean, because it is a clean bird. Did you know that the bird Joseph and Mary offered up when Jesus was born, when they brought the sacrifice to the temple, was a dove?

Therefore, when Noah sent out a dove it returned to the ark because it found no rest; the waters were still on the face of the earth. The dove could only rest upon the just, the clean. Noah waited another week and then sent it out again. This time, it came back with a bitter olive branch in its mouth, the olive branch being a symbol of peace all over the world.

In Genesis 8:11, we see that the dove came to Noah in the evening. Think about this. Jesus was crucified at nine o'clock in the morning, but He died at three o'clock between the Hebrew evenings—the same time the temple sacrifice had to be finished.

> *And he stayed yet other seven days; and sent forth the dove; which returned not again unto him any more.* (Genesis 8:12)

So, the third time Noah sent out the dove, it never returned, because it found a place to rest. Symbolically, it flew all the way to Luke 3:22 and landed upon Jesus. In Luke 3:22, when John the Baptist baptized Jesus, Scripture says,

> *And the Holy Ghost descended in a bodily shape like a dove [like in Genesis 8:9] upon him, and a voice came from heaven, which said, Thou art my beloved Son; in thee I am well pleased.*

As a member of the *body* of Christ, do you understand what this means? This means that God says to you, "*You* are my beloved son, *you* are my beloved daughter, in whom I am well pleased."

SELF-CONDEMNED

So often I have asked why it is that some people in a prayer line receive the anointing while others do not. The anointing flows into them and they receive what they came for. Other people come and the dove can't rest there. The Holy Spirit can't rest on them because they have condemnation going on. Why do some people not get healed? They are self-condemned. Now, the Holy Spirit lives in you when you're born again, but He cannot rest upon you and He can't flow through you like He wants to if you have condemnation.

David somehow understood that. In Psalm 66:18, he said, *"If I regard iniquity in my heart, the Lord will not hear me."* Why? Because such a person can't operate in faith. David understood that the just shall live by faith. How else could David have gone on to be king after what he had done? How could Paul the Apostle say in 2 Corinthians 7:2, *"Receive us; we have wronged no man"*? In 2 Timothy 1:3, he also said that he served God with a pure conscience from his forefathers. He said he wasn't ashamed. How could he say that unless he knew what I'm teaching you right now?

If the Spirit can't rest on you because you're feeling condemned, you need to get over that condemnation—because it attracts the raven. The raven is a type of the anti-Christ spirit. Who else would want to make you feel guilty? The Holy Spirit is called the Comforter, so you know it's not Him. You need to understand when you're feeling that way that there's a raven picking away at your flesh. When that happens, you need to give up all hope in yourself. Just say, "Little I can do all things through big Christ who strengthens me" (Philippians 4:13, paraphrased).

I'm not living another day doing this deal on my own. I'm not going to try anything anymore. I'm done trying. I'm going to be carefree. I can't begin to tell you how much I don't care. You see, I don't want to be a floating corpse.

Isaiah 54:9 says,

> *For this is as the waters of Noah unto me: for as I have sworn that the waters of Noah should no more go over the earth; so have I sworn that I would not be wroth with thee, nor rebuke thee.*

In other words, God is saying, "I promise to tell the truth, the whole truth, and nothing but the truth. So help Me, Me. I will not be angry with you, I will not rebuke you. Adam, you don't have to hide from me. Adam, why are you where you are? Adam, why are you hiding, why are you feeling shame?"

Jesus said in John 3:17 that He didn't come to condemn the world, so if you are being condemned and are a part of this world, where's the condemnation coming from? If it's not Him, there is only one other source. The next time you feel condemned, just picture a big old raven sitting on the top of your head pecking at your skull.

God has made a promise. He is giving you grace for your disgrace. He brought grace. He reversed the curse, just like when the ark landed on that mountain.

For the mountains shall depart, and the hills be removed; but my kindness [the Hebrew word hesed*] shall not depart from thee, neither shall the covenant of my peace be removed, says the Lord that hath mercy [again,* hesed*] on thee. (Isaiah 54:10)*

In the next verse, He says, *"O thou afflicted, tossed with tempest, and not comforted."* That's condemnation. Can you see that? "Oh thou afflicted, you're feeling condemned. You are more aware of your works than His, and that's why you're afflicted!" He said, "You're just like Noah, bobbing in the boat."

Isaiah 54:14 says that we will be established in righteousness. When you're established in righteousness, you'll be free from fear, terror, and oppression. When you're established in Romans 5:17, the gift of righteousness will cause you to reign in life. When you're established in Romans 5:1, you will know that you are justified and made righteous by faith, and only by faith.

Faith is simply what's been done. My faith in Him is what has already been completed. In righteousness, you shall be established and far from oppression, fear, and terror. They won't even come near you. Why? Because that raven can only sit on flesh. He's been sent out and goes about through the earth like a roaring lion seeking whom he may devour, but he can't devour me and he can't devour you.

A FREE MAN

Have you ever had a list? Have you ever said to yourself something like, "Well, I did this right and I tithed there and I gave an offering, so now I'm going to pray for financial blessing." No, what that basically says is that what you did was enough—but again, the curse did not bring poverty; the curse brought condemnation. If I free myself from condemnation, I'm free from the curse, and if I'm free from the curse, then prosperity is mine, healing is mine, and everything I've been believing God for is mine, because there's no condemnation to block it.

Just think about that. How many people have tried to live a good Christian life? They say, "Well, I'm just doing the best I can." Oh really? "Yes. I'm doing my best, Gary." Well, okay, let's just rephrase that. You should be saying, "I'm doing *His* best. I've entered into *His* rest because *He's* done *His* best! I'm just chilling out now." And what if I make a mistake? Well I have 1 John 1:9 to fall back on—I'll be quick to repent and He will be quick to forgive and cleanse me of all unrighteousness.

Acts 3:19 says, "Repent ye therefore, and be converted, that your sins may be blotted out..." My response to the word "repent" here is that I only have one thing to repent of—trusting in myself. I pray Proverbs 3:5–6 all the time. "I trust in You, Lord, with all my heart and lean not on my own way of doing things. I acknowledge You in all my ways and You will direct my steps." It's amazing to me how many times I'll pray that prayer in the morning and then depend on myself all day long.

Despite that, I realize that I can't do it on my own, that I've been crucified with Christ, and that I no longer live but Christ lives in me. The life I now live in the flesh I live by faith (Galatians 2:20). The just shall live by faith (Romans 1:17). It's already been done, so we need to just chill out. We need to relax in the finished work. Just walk worthy of the Lord and receive wisdom and revelation knowledge. Receive grace for disgrace. Remember that anytime you feel afflicted and not comforted, the problem is self-righteousness.

The word self-righteous gives the impression of a pious religious attitude—and to some degree, that's what it is. We associate self-righteousness with someone who has his nose in the air, but sometimes self-righteousness abides in you when you have your head down. Maybe you tried all week to be better than you were the last week, but you just messed up. Maybe you freaked out and acted like an idiot in front of somebody. You see, this is why Paul the Apostle could say in

1 Corinthians 4:3, *"But with me it is a very small thing that I should be judged of you…"* He was saying, "I don't give a rip what you're thinking about me." He didn't care what anybody thought.

This is what I want you to see, in the last part of that verse: *"…I judge not mine own self."* Can you see that? I don't judge me; I'm not my judge. I don't decide at the end of the day whether I did good or whether I didn't do good, because I don't want the raven sitting on top of my head.

Well, Paul didn't care whether anyone judged him or not. It meant very little to him. Ben Campbell Johnson's translation of 1 Corinthians 4:3 says,

> *I am not the least concerned with the fact that you are deciding what is right and what is wrong with me… and even passing sentence on me. Neither you nor anyone else can put me down unless I first put myself down [and I'm not doing that].[1]*

This murderer became a free man! Why shouldn't the church be free?

CONDEMNATION EQUALS SELF-RIGHTEOUSNESS

If you don't remember anything else, just remember this: anytime you're feeling condemned, you are declaring yourself self-righteous. I'm going to say it one more time. Anytime at all that you feel condemned, if you've made Jesus the Lord of your life, you are declaring yourself self-righteous. And if you haven't made Jesus the Lord of your life, Romans 10:9–10 says, you don't confess sin. Christians get to confess sin. Sinners get to confess Jesus, and that's all. I sat in church all my life watching Christians try to get unbelievers saved by saying, "Confess your sins." No. Just read your Bible, which says to confess Jesus! The sin question has been settled, that's why you confess Jesus.

Christians get the opportunity to say, "God, I missed it. Thank You that Your grace is sufficient for me. Lord, I believe through Your strength

---

[1] Johnson, Ben Campbell. *The Heart of Paul: A Relational Paraphrase of the New Testament* (Toccoa, GA: A Great Love, Inc., 1976).

that, as Romans 12:1 says, I submit my body to You a living sacrifice, holy, acceptable unto You, which is my reasonable service. I submit my mind to be renewed so that there will be improvement everyday. But it's not based on what I'm doing; it's based on what God has already done. Amen!"

It's all done. You just need to say that you're done trying and you've entered into His rest. Hallelujah!

RIGHTEOUSNESS IS A FREE GIFT

chapter two

PETER'S EXAMPLE

IN CHAPTER ONE, I BRIEFLY MENTIONED PETER. I WOULD NOW LIKE TO look at his life and teachings in more detail.

We saw that Peter, after denying Jesus three times, went back to his career as a fisherman. Even though he had been called to be a fisher of men, he was sure that his ministry was over because he had failed God. So, just like in Luke 5, he went fishing with a few of the other disciples, and fished almost all night without catching anything. When they returned to shore, Peter found Jesus cooking a meal for him; He was cooking it for Peter specifically.

In order to reconcile someone back to yourself, thereby extending forgiveness to someone who had broken fellowship, the custom of the day was to cook a meal for them. Breaking bread resulted in a person's restoration to friendship, partnership, and intimacy. When Peter saw the meal being cooked, he couldn't wait to row ashore. That's why he dove in and began to swim. He couldn't wait to get there, because he realized he was forgiven. Peter could say, "His grace has come for my disgrace. I was living in shame and guilt, but now I'm totally forgiven and I haven't done anything to earn it." Now, because of this incident, you will understand why Peter wrote so much about grace when you read 1 and 2 Peter.

We also know that the Apostle Paul mentioned grace at least ninety times in his writings. When you read the gospel of John, as well as John's letters, you'll find that he talks mostly about *agape* love—unconditional love. This is because John, being young and in his teens when he met Jesus, didn't have a whole lot of baggage in his life. John was able to focus on the love of the Lord and receive it. He was able to receive that unconditional love whereas Paul struggled with it and had to go through grace. So, as a result, we see that Paul talked about grace a lot, but he got it. He got the message!

Peter also preached grace. In 2 Peter, grace is mentioned at least ten times. Let's look at how Peter finished his course. One of the last things he had to say before his death comes in 2 Peter 3:15:

And account that the longsuffering of our Lord is salvation; even as our beloved brother Paul also according to the wisdom given unto him hath written unto you.

Paul mostly preached grace, probably almost twice as much as he talked about love. This is because he needed it. He had been a murderer; he said that when it came to sinners, he was the chief sinner. He would have been welcome in any of the synagogues before his conversion, but he counted it as dung because he realized that all his rituals hadn't profited him anything.

In 2 Peter 3:16, Peter said that some of these concepts are hard to understand. It's hard to understand that you don't have to do anything. I might have known this intellectually, but while receiving and learning about Christ in Israel I received the revelation that I need to walk in Him (Colossians 2:6). I learned Christ in an alcohol dependency centre when I couldn't do anything to help myself, and that's the way I am to live today. I am to trust Him with all my heart and not lean on my own understanding, or on my own way of doing things, but instead I am to acknowledge Him in all of my ways and believe that He will direct my steps (Proverbs 3:5–6). I don't want to have any confidence in the flesh.

Peter had confidence in his flesh when Jesus said, in Luke 22:31–34, that Satan desired to sift him like wheat. Peter's reply was, "I'm ready, Jesus. I'll even die with you." Jesus said, "No, Peter, you won't. You'll deny me three times because you don't depend on me." Jesus prayed that Peter's faith wouldn't fail, but he knew Peter's faith wasn't in Him as his High Priest, but instead in what Peter himself could do. Hebrews 3:1 says that Jesus is our heavenly High Priest. He is the Apostle and High Priest over our confession, of His Word, and He watches over His Word to perform it (Jeremiah 1:12).

RIGHTEOUSNESS IS A FREE GIFT

So, Jesus is watching over you and He lives forever to be your intercessor (Hebrews 7:25). You have someone praying for you today (Romans 8:34). Somebody might say that they'll pray for you, then walk away and forget all about it, but let me tell you that you have somebody who's praying for you all the time. That dove, representing the Holy Spirit, cannot land on someone who's condemned. It has to find the just—those who are justified by faith (Romans 5:1) and have right standing with the Father through the Lord Jesus Christ.

You have to understand that you've been justified by faith, and not by anything you did. You were made righteous by faith. Romans 1:17 says that the righteousness of God came from a revelation that the just shall live by faith. When you realize that righteousness is a gift from God, you also realize that God made Jesus *to be sin for us, who knew no sin; that we would be made the righteousness of God in Him"* (2 Corinthians 5:21). When we accept His righteousness and the fact that we are in Him, and when we receive prayer for healing, we won't be basing healing on our performance but on the completed work at the cross (1 Peter 2:24). It is grace, plus or minus nothing! We must accept

17

what He did and not trust in the things we do. The life I now live in the flesh, I live by faith in the Son of God. I've been crucified with Christ. I no longer live, but now Christ lives in me (Galatians 2:20). That's what Paul said. So, you've got to let Christ live in you. You can't depend on yourself.

In 2 Peter 3:17–18, Peter says,

> *Ye therefore, beloved, seeing ye know these things before, beware lest ye also, being led away with the error of the wicked, fall from your own steadfastness. But grow in grace, and in the knowledge of our Lord and Saviour Jesus Christ. To him be glory both now and for ever. Amen.*

These are the last words Peter wrote.

ESCAPE CORRUPTION

Let's go back and see how Peter started this letter. In verse one, he began by saying,

> *Simon Peter, a servant and an apostle of Jesus Christ, to them that have obtained like precious faith [the same faith Peter used to walk on the water, the same faith you have] with us through the righteousness of God and our Saviour Jesus Christ: Grace and peace be multiplied unto you through the knowledge of God, and of Jesus our Lord, according as his divine power hath given unto us all things that pertain unto life and godliness [your physical life and spiritual life], through the knowledge of him that hath called us to glory and virtue [not misery and suffering]: whereby are given unto us exceeding great and precious promises: that by these ye might be partakers of the divine nature, having escaped the corruption that is in the world through lust.* (2 Peter 1:1–4)

Notice here that he said you can escape the corruption of this world by hanging onto the promises of God, not by hanging onto what you can do. He then demonstrates in the rest of the chapter that once

18

you're operating in faith, you're going to take that faith and add moral excellence. You're not going to do that by a system of rules; you'll do it by depending on God, just like you received salvation.

Peter then tells you how by faith you add brotherly kindness, *agape* love, and the whole process. But you also need to notice that it is a process, a process of growing up in God. You don't struggle to grow up. Did you ever see a child struggling to grow up? No. Through food and physical development, natural growth occurs which involves no struggle. Growing up in God requires the natural growth process, only with a steady diet of God's Word, hearing, and doing. You grow your faith by acting on it. That's it!

In the book of Romans, Paul used the word grace twenty-four times. Romans 3:20 says,

> *Therefore by the deeds of the law [by keeping the law or the commandments, by how good I can act] there shall no flesh be justified in his sight: for by the law is the knowledge of sin.*

This is simply Galatians 3:24 written another way, the law being a schoolmaster who brings you to Christ to make you realize that you can't do this in and of yourself. You probably can't even recite six of the Ten Commandments, let alone do them.

YOU CAN'T EARN IT

According to Romans 3:21–22,

> *But now the righteousness of God without the law is manifested, being witnessed by the law and the prophets; even the righteousness of God which is by faith of Jesus Christ unto all...*

The whole world has been offered the gift of righteousness, but it comes upon all who will believe it and receive it. If you receive grace for disgrace, you will be free forever! Paul had such a revelation in 2 Corinthians 7:2, where he said, *"Receive us; we have wronged no man."* In 2 Timothy 1:3, he said, *"I thank God, whom I serve from my forefathers with pure conscience."* In verse twelve, he said, *"I am not ashamed."* He had no shame in his life. He had a pure conscience.

How do you have a pure conscience? You accept God's grace!

Now here's the key. When you and I get into works, we are self-righteous. We think of self-righteous people as being pious, but no, someone who's self-righteous is someone who thinks they can do it themselves. *"I* can do this. *I* can live a better Christian life today than I did yesterday. Just watch *me."* No. Say it this way: "I can live a better Christian life today. Just watch Him." Then you are free! Every day, we must make a decision. We're not dependent on ourselves at all. We are dependent on Him.

> *Even the righteousness of God which is by faith of [in] Jesus Christ unto all and upon all them that believe: for there is no difference: for all have sinned, and come short of the glory of God; being justified freely by his grace...* (Romans 3:22–24)

The Greek word used here for "freely" is *dorean*, which means without cost, without cause, without condition. In other words, righteousness isn't something you can earn; it's free. If someone gives you something for free and you try to pay them for it, then it's not free.

In the Ben Campbell Johnson translation, Romans 3:23 reads, *"...all of us have gotten off the track of God's original intention and have missed the fulfillment for which we were destined."*[2] But thank God for the next verse—*"being justified freely..."* In other words, there's nothing I can do. I am justified by His grace through the redemption that is in Christ Jesus, who was made to be the propitiation (the act of making satisfaction for any crime) for our sins. So, when I was down in the pit, He pulled me out.

> *Being justified freely by his grace through the redemption that is in Christ Jesus: whom God hath set forth to be a propitiation through faith in his blood, to declare his righteousness for the remission of sins that are past, through the forbearance of God; to declare, I say,*

---

[2] Ibid.

at this time his righteousness: that he might be just, and the justifier
of him which believeth in Jesus. (Romans 3:24–26)

So what is Paul saying here? He's saying that there's no crime against you. He's saying what he said in Colossians 2:14, that God destroyed the ordinances and the things that were written against you by nailing them to His cross. Your penalty was paid in full!

The worst part of Jesus' day on the cross was at high noon when He cried out, "My God, My God, why have you forsaken me?" Of the seven things He said, that was number four, and it was the worst one because it was the only time that He didn't call His Father "Father," but instead "God." This is when my sin came on Him. Experiencing my sin was worse than the crucifixion. If He was willing to pay that price, surely I can enjoy my liberty! No one is ever going to put me back into any religious cage! I'm not looking for a reason to sin; I'm looking for a reason to live right. When you know how much He loves you, you just love Him back. When you just hang out with Him, the garbage and baggage in your life just leaves.

WHERE IS BOASTING?

[Jesus was made] a propitiation through faith in his blood, to declare
his righteousness for the remission of sins that are past, through the
forbearance of God; to declare, I say, at this time his righteousness:
that he might be just, and the justifier of him which believeth in
Jesus. Where is boasting then? (Romans 3:25–27)

I can't go to God and say, "Lord, I'm the pastor of the church and I tithe and I give offerings and I send money to Kenneth Copeland and Bill Winston." I don't need to wag that out in front of God. It won't profit me any. None of that would have happened if He hadn't saved me. I wasn't giving to any ministries before He came into my life, so there's no point in bragging now. He prompts your heart and you obey His promptings, that's all.

Where is boasting then? It is excluded. By what law? of works?
Nay: but by the law of faith. Therefore we conclude that a man is
justified by faith without the deeds of the law. (Romans 3:27–28)

You are justified by faith, not by trying to act holy! Holiness is not a
system of rules; holiness is who God is. So when He tells us to become
holy in 1 Peter 1:16 (the Greek word for "holy" here is *ginomai*), He's
saying, "Grow up in Me. Be changed from glory to glory into the image
of Jesus." You're just growing up in Him. It's not some pious way that
you act anymore, because righteousness would then be a system of rules.
Righteousness is a gift from God.

What shall we say then that Abraham our father, as pertaining
to the flesh, hath found? For if Abraham were justified by works,
he hath whereof to glory [he would be able to brag]; but not
before God. For what saith the scripture? Abraham believed God
[referring to Genesis 15:6], and it was counted unto him for
righteousness. Now to him that worketh is the reward not reckoned
of grace, but of debt [which is pretty plain to see]. But to him that
worketh not [doesn't do the works of the law], but believeth on him
that justifieth the ungodly, his faith is counted for righteousness.
(Romans 4:1–5)

I love the next verse here. It's about David, who on his worst day,
killed Uriah, the Hittite.

Even as David also describeth the blessedness of the man, unto
whom God imputeth righteousness without works, saying, Blessed
are they whose iniquities are forgiven [that's me], and whose sins
are covered [that's me]. Blessed is the man to whom the Lord will
not impute sin [that's me]. (Romans 4:6–8)

It's you and me whose sins are covered. That's us. You are blessed
and I am blessed! Ben Campbell Johnson's translation says,

The psalmist David described the happiness of everyone who has a right relationship with God without trying to achieve it by keeping the rules: "How happy are the persons whose breaches of the rules are forgiven, whose disobedience to God is overlooked! How happy they are who don't have their misdeeds counted against them by God!" (Romans 4:6-8)[3]

MUCH MORE!

Romans 5:17 is so powerful. In it, Paul said that death reigned by one man's sin, Adam's offense. But then he said that if you think death produced something, you haven't seen anything yet!

For if by one man's offence death reigned by one; much more they which receive abundance of grace and of the gift of righteousness shall reign in life by one, Jesus Christ. (Romans 5:17)

"Much more they which receive." You need to circle "receive" in your Bible. You need to receive this. It won't just fall off you like an apple falls off a tree. You have to receive this. You need to reach out and take it; it's been offered to you! He said, *"Much more they which receive abundance of grace"* (emphasis mine). "Much more" and "abundance" are big words coming from a big God. Grace is not in scarce supply. There is an abundance of grace and righteousness; that's how you are to reign in life!

You might say to yourself, "I'm just an old sinner saved by grace." No, you're not. You're the righteousness of God in Christ.

IT'S FREE

Righteousness is a gift. When you receive the gift of righteousness, then and only then will you be able to reign in life. Why? David said it this way in Psalms 66:18—*"If I regard iniquity in my heart, the Lord will not hear me."* He didn't say "if *God* regards iniquity in my heart..." He said, "If *I* regard iniquity in my heart..." Why? Because we can't pray in faith when we're feeling guilt. When we feel condemnation and when we feel shame, we can't operate in faith.

---

[3] Ibid.

If you get a hold of this truth—that righteousness is by faith, not based on your works but on what He's done—then you can reign in life. Then you can pray with confidence. Then you can be expecting. You didn't do anything to earn your salvation and you can't do anything to earn any relationship with God now. God is the One who moved from heaven to earth. He is the One who went down into that hole in Caiaphas' basement. He is the One who went to hell and took the keys of death, hell, and the grave. He is the One who rose far above all principalities and power, might, dominion, and every other name.

In Ephesians 2:6, God said that He raised us up together with Him and we are seated in the heavenly realm in Christ. He raised you up to sit with Him! This is why He said in Hebrews 4:16, *"Come boldly unto the throne of grace, that [you] may obtain mercy, and find grace to help in time of need."* When? When you have it all together? No, to help you in your time of need, when you don't have it all together. That's when He said to come boldly to Him. When you failed and when you fall down, come into the office, the throne room of grace, to the Creator of the universe, and He'll say, "Hey! I love you! Come on, let's just turn this thing around. Let's repent and get back at it again. Don't quit just because you fell down." Falling down isn't the same thing as failing!

NO CONDEMNATION

Romans 8:1 tells us that there is no condemnation to those who are *in Christ Jesus.* That's you and me! Adam, when he sinned, ran and hid because he was naked and ashamed. He tried to cover himself with some religious deal, but God says there's no condemnation. He doesn't want you to run and hide from Him; He wants you to come boldly into the throne room of grace to obtain His mercy.

No condemnation means that there's no accusing, nagging voice irritating us. If we have an accusing, nagging voice, we know it's not from the Comforter, the Holy Ghost. It's the accuser of the brethren, and he's a liar and the father of lies. So, whatever he's telling you is a lie. Jesus said that the truth isn't even in him. If he tells you that you're not going to make it, you can be sure of one thing—you will make it. If he tells you that you're going under this time, know for sure that you're going over!

WALK THE WORD

It takes a decision to live the spirit life. You must decide to walk in the spirit and not fulfill the lust of the flesh. Romans 8:14 says that the sons of God are as many as are led by the Spirit of God. In John 6:63, Jesus said it this way: *"The words that I speak unto you, they are spirit, and they are life."* Walking in the Word is the key. Just like in 2 Corinthians 5:7, walking by faith and not by sight isn't mysterious. It requires us to walk by what the Word says and not by what we see, feel, taste, touch, or smell.

So if my body says I'm sick but the Word says I'm healed, what am I going to do? Go around and say how sick I am? No, I'm going to say, "By the stripes of Jesus, I am healed and made whole." Someone may tell you that you don't look whole. Stay away from people who are going to drag you down. You need to be around people who want to build you up, believe in you, and encourage you.

Why do we hang around people who see us get a little leverage and then try to yank us down? I'm reminded of a visit to Hong Kong with friends who ordered crab at a restaurant. The waiter brought out a dirty old bucket with live crabs crawling around inside. If you have only one crab in a bucket you must keep the lid on because it will crawl out. If you have more than one crab you can take the lid off and sit it right there on the floor, because as soon as one gets almost all the way out, the other one will pull it back in. The same principle applies to some of our friends. They're comfortable with us where we are right now, beside them. If you start to grow, they might want to pull you down. Those people have been there too long; you can pray for them from a distance.

You need people to encourage you and believe in you. God believes in you! He says, *"Greater is he that is in you, than he that is in the world [your circumstances]"* (1 John 4:4). God says you're His heir, a joint heir with Him (Romans 8:17). Who will separate you from the love of God? (Romans 8:35) Nothing and no one! When God shows up, the first thing He says is, "Don't be afraid. Don't be dismayed. Everything is going to be cool."

STAND STILL

In 2 Chronicles 20:15, He said that the battle isn't yours, but God's. That's grace! God said, "All I want you to do, people of Judah, is praise Me. Go down and stand still, and I will show you the salvation of your Lord."

At Jericho, in Joshua 6, He told the people of Israel not to say a word until the seventh day. Then he wanted them to shout and praise. The hardest thing a Christian will ever do is stand still, but when you stand still you realize that it's not about your works.

So often we try to fix the messes we're in, but the best way to fix it is to have ourselves a hallelujah fit! Just begin to praise God… dance around your bedroom, do whatever you have to do. Just say, "No, I'm not participating in this. I'm going to enjoy hanging around with God. He says He's going to fight my battles for me. I'm not even dependent on my faith in Him, because even that is a gift from God. It's not of works, lest anyone should boast."

WALK IN THE SPIRIT

There is therefore now no condemnation to them which are in Christ Jesus, who walk not after the flesh, but after the Spirit. For the law of the Spirit of life [Romans 3:27 calls it the law of faith] hath made me free from the law of sin and death. (Romans 8:1–2)

That's it. We just need to make a decision to walk by what He says. Romans 8:4–6 tells us,

That the righteousness of the law might be fulfilled in us, who walk not after the flesh, but after the Spirit. For they that are after the flesh do mind the things of the flesh; but they that are after the Spirit the things of the Spirit. For to be carnally minded [or to be sense-led] is death [not meaning to fall over dead, but to be separated from the blessing]; but to be spiritually minded is life and peace.

Romans 8:8 says those who are led by the flesh cannot please God. Why? Because Hebrews 11:6 tells us that without faith it's impossible to please God. Money is your currency here on earth; faith is your currency in heaven. If you're not operating in faith, you cannot please God because He can't bless you.

It's not like He isn't pleased with you. Unbelief doesn't please Him because it makes it impossible for Him to bless you. God's grace is always abounding toward you. He is forever seeking you out! When you read James 4, you'll see how He boils over with jealousy for you! He wants to be with you so much that if you give Him an hour of your day, He'll be back asking for two—just because He wants to be with you. The way He feels for you is just like you might feel toward a child or parent. You have no idea how much more God feels toward you. David tried to describe it in Psalm 139:17–18. He said that if he knew the thoughts God had toward him, they would be more than the sand. Not the sand of one beach... the thoughts that God had toward one man is greater than *all* the sand in the world.

FAITH BRINGS GRACE

Romans 11:6 is so powerful! As I scrolled through the verses about grace, I found "grace" four times in this one verse.

And if by grace, then is it no more of works: otherwise grace is no more grace. But if it be of works, then is it no more grace: otherwise work is no more work.

What Paul means here is that grace isn't determined by human actions. Grace doesn't come by being good enough or it wouldn't be free. It's not based on your performance; it's based on what He's already done.

Who would have ever thought that trying to keep the Ten Commandments would put you under a curse? Not by breaking them, but by trying to keep them! Yet this is what Paul taught the Galatians. He said, "Foolish Galatians, who has bewitched you? You guys are trying to go back under the law after you've been saved by grace through faith." Galatians 3:12–13 says,

> *And the law is not of faith: but, The man that doeth them shall live*
> *in them [and be judged by it, unfortunately]. Christ hath redeemed*
> *us from the curse of the law…*

What is the curse of the law again? Condemnation! God asked, "Adam, where are you?" The answer: "I'm hiding because I'm ashamed. I found myself naked, so I'm trying to cover myself." That's what religion does; it tries to cover up. No. You see, Christ has redeemed us from the curse that brings condemnation and fear. Faith that's been perverted then turns into fear and brings condemnation. Fear will bring disgrace just like faith will hook into His grace. If I'm feeling condemned, I know that I've put myself under the law and under a curse. I don't want to be under a curse. I've been redeemed from the curse and I need to stay over in faith.

> *Christ hath redeemed us from the curse of the law, being made a*
> *curse for us: for it is written, Cursed is every one that hangeth on*
> *a tree: That the blessing of Abraham might come on the Gentiles*
> *[that's me] through Jesus Christ; that we [that's you and I] might*
> *receive the promise of the Spirit through faith.* (Galatians 3:13–
> 14)

WHO'S TALKING TO YOU?

The woman at the well in John 4 said, "We worship at this mountain, they worship at that mountain." She had all the rituals down, but Jesus said, "You don't understand the gift of God and who it is who's talking to you. I know you've been married five times, and I know that the guy you're living with right now isn't your husband." But He didn't say all that in one judgmental, condemning word! Just like in John 8:11, when Jesus spoke to the woman who was caught in adultery, He said, "Neither do I condemn you."

When you know you're not condemned, you can go and sin no more—and you can be free. As long as you feel condemned, you're going to keep failing and just keep falling. Jesus told the woman at the well, "You don't know the gift of God and the one sitting here talking to you. None of those men satisfied you, because you were trying to fill a spiritual need with a physical thing."

Some people try to get comfort by going to the fridge until they get so big they can hardly move, and we judge them for it. We should never judge them. They're trying to satisfy a spiritual need with something physical. That's all it is. This woman was simply trying to satisfy the emptiness she felt, the separation from righteousness she was experiencing, by getting another man. Jesus said, "If you'll drink the water that I have, it will spring up into everlasting life and you'll never thirst again! You'll never have to feed yourself something physical to satisfy a spiritual need."

After speaking with her, He stayed two more days. And for two thousand years He stayed with the Gentile church so that you would understand the grace that He was preaching.

NOT JUSTIFIED BY THE LAW

> *For as many as are of the works of the law are under the curse: for it is written, Cursed is every one that continueth not in all things which are written in the book of the law to do them.* (Galatians 3:10)

Wow! What a thing to say, that when you try to keep the law you feel condemned, and when you feel condemned you declare your own self-righteousness. Remember Romans 10:3? The Jews were ignorant of His righteousness, which is by faith, so they went about trying to establish their own righteousness, saying, "Who can bring Jesus down? Who can raise Jesus up?" Paul said, "No, the Word of God is near you, even in your mouth and in your heart. It's the word of faith we preach. I am the righteousness of God in Christ, and that shouldn't irritate you—because you are, too."

Let's read this same verse out of the Amplified version:

> *And all who depend on the Law [who are seeking to be justified by obedience to the Law of rituals] are under a curse and doomed to disappointment and destruction, for it is written in the Scriptures,*

Cursed (accursed, devoted to destruction, doomed to eternal punishment) be everyone who does not continue to abide (live and remain) by all the precepts and commands written in the Book of the Law and to practice them. Now it is evident that no person is justified (declared righteous and brought into right standing with God) through the Law, for the Scripture says, The man in right standing with God [the just, the righteous] shall live by and out of faith and he who through and by faith is declared righteous and in right standing with God shall live. (Galatians 3:10–11, AMP)

Galatians 3:11–12, in the King James, says,

But that no man is justified by the law in the sight of God, it is evident: for, The just shall live by faith. And the law is not of faith: but, The man that doeth them shall live in them.

I don't want to live by the law. I want to live by grace and through faith.

Knowing that a man is not justified by the works of the law, but by the faith of Jesus Christ, even we have believed in Jesus Christ, that we might be justified by the faith of Christ, and not by the works of the law [our works]: for by the works of the law [our works] shall no flesh be justified. (Galatians 2:16)

Therefore being justified by faith, we have peace with God through our Lord Jesus Christ: by whom also we have access by faith into this grace wherein we stand, and rejoice in hope of the glory of God. And not only so, but we glory in tribulations also: knowing that tribulation worketh patience; and patience, experience; and experience, hope: and hope maketh not ashamed; because the love of God is shed abroad in our hearts by the Holy Ghost which is given unto us. For when we were yet without strength, in due time Christ died for the ungodly. For scarcely for a righteous man will one die: yet peradventure for a good man some would even dare to die. But

God commendeth [commanded] his love toward us, in that, while we were yet sinners [my worst day as a drug addict], Christ died for us [me]. Much more [here it is again, much more*] then, being now justified by his blood, we shall be saved from wrath through him.* (Romans 5:1–9)

God has shown us time and again throughout His Word that we are to live by faith. We are justified by His blood and not by our own works or by the keeping of the law.

PAUL'S LETTER OF RIGHTEOUSNESS

chapter three

PAUL'S LETTER

WHEN YOU READ THE BOOK OF ROMANS, YOU CAN'T JUST PULL OUT A single piece of it, because Paul starts a theme in chapter one and carries it all the way through to the end of the book. If you look at the context of the whole book, you'll be totally liberated, totally free!

But over the years, people haven't done that. They've extracted certain verses, like Romans 3:23 (*"For all have sinned, and come [fallen] short of the glory of God"*). Yes, but please tell me the next verses! I remember walking out of church as a young Christian feeling like a dog because I didn't know the next verse— *"Being justified freely by his grace through the redemption that is in Christ Jesus"* (Romans 3:24). They didn't tell me I was justified freely by His grace! I went in feeling pretty good and went home feeling miserable, thinking there was something wrong with this. Romans can't be separated! If this book alone was the only book you had, you could live a happy Christian life.

Grace for Disgrace

In Romans 1, Paul says that the gospel is the power of God, a righteous revelation.

> For I am not ashamed of the gospel [good news] of Christ [the anointed one and His anointing]: for it [this good news] is the power of God unto salvation to every one that believeth; to the Jew first, and also to the Greek. For therein [in this good news] is the righteousness of God revealed [or a revelation of righteousness] from faith to faith: as it is written, The just shall live by faith. (Romans 1:16–17)

Notice that Paul says "from faith to faith" and not "from works to works." Here's something that I learned from this verse: I must give up trust in myself in order to have faith in God. Would you like to know why people struggle with faith? They may know the seven steps, and they may have read all the teachings of many anointed preachers, but still they don't have even a drop of faith. It's because they still have faith in themselves.

In order to have faith in God, I have to give up all faith in my own works. I need to give up faith in Gary in order to operate in faith in God. A righteous man will live by faith, a life of righteousness, because it has its source in God alone.

Think for a minute about what Martin Luther saw. He saw the clergy going up and down the steps in Rome, just like they do today, until their knees were bloody. I saw a woman doing that very thing in Montreal one day. This little old lady's knees were bloody from climbing the stairs of the basilica on top of Mount Royal. She was trying to find God, which is no different than being at the Western Wall and watching Rachel weeping for her children (Jeremiah 40:1, Matthew 2:18).

Martin Luther watched this taking place. One day, he heard the Lord say, "The just shall live by faith," and it revolutionized his life! Martin Luther spoke of the importance of God's word by saying,

> This letter [referring to the book of Romans] is truly the most important piece in the New Testament. It is purest Gospel. It is

well worth a Christian's while not only to memorize it word for word but also to occupy himself with it daily, as though it were the daily bread of the soul… the way it is with human laws: you satisfy the demands of the law with works, whether your heart is in it or not… God judges what is in the depths of the heart. Therefore his law also makes demands on the depths of the heart and doesn't let the heart rest content in works… The works of the law are everything that a person does or can do of his own free will and by his own powers to obey the law. But because in doing such works the heart abhors the law and yet is forced to obey it, the works are a total loss and are completely useless… But to fulfill the law means to do its work eagerly, lovingly and freely… That is why faith alone makes someone just and fulfills the law… Faith is a living, unshakeable confidence in God's grace; it is so certain, that someone would die a thousand times for it. This kind of trust in and knowledge of God's grace makes a person joyful, confident, and happy…[4]

I'm surrendered to God. Like Paul said, "I am what I am by the grace of God" (1 Corinthians 15:10, paraphrased). If you don't like me now, stick around, because I'm changing. But it's not me changing me; It's Him changing me, He that works in and through me both to will and to do His good pleasure (Philippians 2:13). Just let Him do the work!

How many people have run away from God and the church because they thought, *I can't do it. I just keep falling and I feel like a failure around other Christians. I can't stand it.* They don't verbalize it, but they disappear from church one after another because they've never gotten rid of condemnation, guilt, and shame.

---

[4] "*Vorrede auff die Epistel S. Paul: an die Romer*" in D. Martin Luther: *Die gantze Heilige Schrifft Deudsch 1545 aufs new zurericht*, ed. Hans Volz and Heinz Blanke (Munich: Roger & Bernhard, 1972), Vol. 2, pp. 2254–2268. Preface to the Letter of St. Paul to the Romans: by Martin Luther, 1483–1546. Translated by Bro. Andrew Thornton, OSB.

NO RESPECTER OF PERSONS

Romans 2 is written to the religious man, indicating that righteousness doesn't come from human effort. It is like someone *trying to be.* How many times have you witnessed somebody and heard them say, "Well, I'm a good person"? They very well could be a good, moral person, but human good isn't divine good and is described by the prophet Isaiah as filthy rags (Isaiah 64:6).

Let's look at the first few verses in chapter two.

Therefore thou art inexcusable, O man, whosoever thou art that judgest [judges someone else]: for wherein thou judgest another, thou condemnest thyself; for thou that judgest doest the same things. But we are sure that the judgment of God is according to truth against them which commit such things. And thinkest thou this, O man, that judgest them which do such things, and doest the same, that thou shalt escape the judgment of God? Or despisest thou the riches of his goodness and forbearance and longsuffering; not knowing that the goodness of God leadeth thee to repentance? (Romans 2:1–4, emphasis mine)

Romans 2:11 tells us that *"there is no respect of persons with God."* In Acts 10:34, when Peter went over to Cornelius' house, he arrived and was ready to preach. Peter said, *"Of a truth I perceive that God is no respecter of persons."* This was already written down in Deuteronomy 10:17, which says, *"For the LORD your God is God of gods, and Lord of lords... which regardeth not persons..."*

That's good news! The good news is that He respects faith. He's not looking at your flesh, He doesn't respect personalities, and He doesn't love one personality more than another. If somebody is very charismatic and extroverted while someone else is more introverted, it doesn't matter with God, because what God respects is their faith.

JUSTIFIED FREELY

Romans 3:24–25 says that we were freely justified.

Being justified freely by his grace through the redemption that is in Christ Jesus: Whom God hath set forth to be a propitiation through faith in his blood, to declare his righteousness for the remission of sins that are past, through the forbearance of God.

I was justified freely by His grace! Jesus was made to be propitiation, the act of making satisfaction for any crime. So when I was down in the pit, He pulled me out.

David had a revelation that he was freely justified when he wrote Psalms 40:2. *"He brought me up also out of an horrible pit, out of the miry clay, and set my feet upon a rock."* David saw some things in the spirit, just like Abraham did. The Bible says that Abraham rejoiced to see Jesus' day. He saw it and he was glad (John 8:56). He saw it before he ever offered up Isaac. He saw the death, burial, and resurrection of the Lord Jesus. He saw it in his mind, and somehow he knew that God, His Covenant Partner, was going to give us His own Son. It took Abraham thirty years to get to know that. How long have you been saved? You probably need to cut yourself a little slack.

Again we need to read Romans 3:24–27.

Being justified freely by his grace through the redemption that is in Christ Jesus: whom God hath set forth to be a propitiation through faith in his blood, to declare his righteousness for the remission of sins that are past, through the forbearance of God; to declare, I say, at this time his righteousness: that he might be just, and the justifier of him which believeth in Jesus [that's me and you]. Where is boasting then? It is excluded. By what law? of works? Nay: but by the law of faith.

You're going to see that law of faith again in Romans 8:1–2, where we read,

There is therefore now no condemnation to them which are in Christ Jesus, who walk not after the flesh, but after the Spirit. [Why?] For the law of the Spirit of life in Christ Jesus hath made me free from the law of sin and death."

That's the law of faith. He's talking about the law of the spirit of life in Christ Jesus.

IT'S ALL ABOUT HIM

Romans 4 is about what Jesus did, and not what I'm doing.

For what saith the scripture? Abraham believed God [which made him righteous], and it was counted unto him for righteousness. (Romans 4:3)

Paul is trying to show you that righteousness doesn't come by keeping the law, by making the point that Abraham believed God before the law was ever given and it was counted unto him for righteousness.

Now to him that worketh is the reward not reckoned of grace, but of debt. (Romans 4:4)

This is like when you want to give somebody something and they try to pay you back. All of a sudden, it's not a gift anymore.

But to him that worketh not, but believeth on him that justifieth the ungodly, his faith is counted for righteousness. (Romans 4:5)

This is why religious people get so mad at people who live by faith. They ask, "You mean, I don't have to do anything?" No, please don't! Don't do anything unless you're led by God, and if you're led by God you'll be led by peace. If you're feeling anxious, you're being pushed, and that comes through the devil.

The Holy Spirit leads you and guides you into all truth (John 16:13). Goodness and mercy will follow you all the days of your life. His rod and His staff will comfort you (Psalm 23). Come on, you're walking along with Him. He who dwells in the secret place of the Most High shall abide in the shadow of the Almighty (Psalm 91:1). There's nothing to be scared about there. He'll lead you into a place of prayer, where He needs you to go.

God speaks of Abraham through the Apostle Paul in Romans 4:5,

But to him that worketh not, but believeth on him that justifieth the ungodly, his faith is counted [to make him right with God] for righteousness.

Abraham didn't need to pray five hours to be right with God; he simply had to believe. Enoch walked with God and *"was not"* when God took him. You see, faith did that. We see in Genesis 5:24 that by faith Enoch walked with God and *"was not."* Not by works, but by faith, for the Lord took him. He just got caught up in God. He got so caught up in God that he wasn't doing something because he had to do it. We tend to think, *I gotta pray, I gotta read my Bible, I gotta, gotta, gotta.* No. Enoch said, "I just want to hang with You today."

Even as David also describeth the blessedness of the man, unto whom God imputeth righteousness without works, saying, Blessed [empowered to prosper] are they whose iniquities are forgiven, and whose sins are covered. Blessed is the man to whom the Lord will not impute sin. (Romans 4:6–8)

Here's what Ben Campbell Johnson said in Romans 4:6–8:

The psalmist David described the happiness of everyone who has a right relationship with God without trying to achieve it by keeping the rules: How happy are the persons whose breaches of the rules are forgiven, whose disobedience to God is overlooked! How happy they are who don't have their misdeeds counted against them by God![5]

How happy are those people? You see, if you aren't happy, if you're not a happy Christian, you aren't doing it right. You are *doing* it instead of *resting* in what He's already done.

---

[5] Johnson, Ben Campbell. *The Heart of Paul: A Relational Paraphrase of the New Testament* (Toccoa, GA: A Great Love, Inc., 1976).

Again, I need to come to the place where I don't have any faith in myself. In my personal life, I had to come to that place as I learned about Christ in a drug dependency centre. I couldn't help myself then, and I can't help myself now. All I have are my senses, which I can exercise to discern both good and evil (Hebrews 5:14). I do know some things that I didn't know before, but if I ever become dependent on what I know, that knowledge will puff up the flesh and make me proud.

PEACE WITH GOD

In Romans 5, we see that we have access and justification by faith. *"Therefore being justified [made righteous] by faith, we have peace with God through Jesus Christ: By whom also we have access by faith into this grace wherein we stand…"* (Romans 5:1–2). That means He's not out to get me. Paul said it another way and I paraphrase: "He apprehended me. I'm already in His grip and now I'm out to apprehend Him, to make His reality my reality. I just want to know Him so His reality will become my reality that I can know Him and the power He purchased for me through His resurrection" (Philippians 3).

> *Therefore being justified [made righteous] by faith, we have peace with God through our Lord Jesus Christ: by whom also we have access by faith into this grace wherein we stand, and rejoice in hope of the glory of God.* (Romans 5:1–2)

When I come into the presence of God, I never see a sign saying "Access Denied." As a matter of fact, if the universe had to shut down for me to get a visitation, that's what would happen for me, and the same thing for you (Joshua 10:2). Everything that you see out there was created for one reason—to get your attention. (Romans 1:20)

I remember when my wife Nancy and I watched a mother and father duck walk up onto the street with their little ducklings. They came down along the curb and up our driveway, then walked along the sidewalk right to our front door. I opened up the door and said, "How are you doing?" They were just over for a visit. After they stayed a little while, they turned around and returned by the exact same route.

Another time, we were walking through the park when we saw one squirrel chasing another squirrel. The one in the rear all of a sudden stopped, looked up at me, and ran right up my leg. When those things happen, that's God! God will speak to you even when you stop and look at a sunrise.

Another time, we walked along a pathway in Israel and saw some tiny flowers. I got down and looked at them, noting the extraordinary detail. We were off somewhere remote, so chances are I may have been the only person to ever see those particular flowers. But God said that all creation declares the glory of God. That's what the flowers—all the small things—are there for; the universe is in place to declare His glory.

Everything exists to get your attention. That is His entire motivation for creation. His grace abounds toward you. Picture somebody running toward you who desperately wants to embrace you. Think about the wayward son who spent all his inheritance over in some place like Vegas. When he came back, the Bible says that while he was still a good distance away his old man saw him and ran to him (Luke 15:20). That's the heart of God! God put those stories in the Bible so that after a while we could figure out that He's not mad at us; He actually likes us.

Romans 5:1–2 sounds like it's saying we should be happy in our Christian walk, rejoicing in the hope of the glory of God. You know why most Christians aren't happy? It's because they're still trying to do everything themselves. Instead of *being* it, they're still trying to *work* it. You are a Christian *being,* not a Christian *doing.*

If God leads you into something, just let Him go. Just follow Him and it will be easy. In Matthew 11:28, He said,

> *Come unto me, all ye that labour and are heavy laden, and I will give you rest. Take my yoke upon you, and learn of me; for I am meek and lowly in heart: and ye shall find rest unto your souls. For my yoke is easy, and my burden is light.*

If it's not easy or light, it's not God. I'm trying to give you some good news, so let it in. Why would people want to resist this? It makes no sense to me. They go home, watch the ten o'clock news, and say to themselves, *Wow, I'd better pray for the world.* Well, I've got the very latest news, and guess what? We win! We need to be watching GNN—God's News Network!

MUCH MORE

We need to look at Romans 5:17, which says,

> *For if by one man's offence [that's Adam] death reigned by one; much more they which receive [you just have to receive it] abundance of grace and of the gift of righteousness shall reign in life by one, Jesus Christ.*

Say it with me: "Much more. Not a little bit more, but much more!" Lots of Christians haven't yet received this, not a thimble full of grace. No. When you receive the abundance of grace and the gift of righteousness you shall reign in life. Why? Because no one can mess you up.

Now, you don't need to have a position of great stature. Your job is what you do, not who you are. What you do is not who you are. Who you are is a joint heir with Jesus (Romans 8:17). Who you are is the righteousness of God in Christ. That's your identity! Don't keep it a secret. Who are you? You are the blood-bought, Holy-Ghost-taught, spirit-filled, tongue-talking, devil-chasing son of the Most High God. That's who you are. Well, you may say I don't have enough education. But get this—God's Word is all the education you'll ever need!

COMPLETE IN HIM

Just like the medians and lines on the highway are there for your safety, Romans 6 is also written to provide boundaries for your protection. Romans 6:12–14 says,

> *Let not sin therefore reign in your mortal body; that ye should obey it in the lusts thereof. Neither yield ye your members as instruments of unrighteousness unto sin: but yield yourselves unto God, as those*

that are alive from the dead, and your members as instruments of righteousness unto God. For sin shall not have dominion over you: for ye are not under the law, but under grace.

Sin won't have dominion over you because you're not under the law; you're under grace. If you won't take condemnation when you make mistakes, condemnation can't work against you and the enemy has nothing to use against you. He'll be saying, "I worked on you for two years to get you in that mess, and then you just asked God to forgive you and you moved on without even getting upset. I better go bother somebody else." All of a sudden, your life is peaceful. Come on! The devil is dumb, but he's not stupid enough to keep hanging around if it's not working. He'll go somewhere else where he can gain access. So send him down the road.

But God be thanked, that ye were the servants of sin, but ye have obeyed from the heart that form of doctrine which was delivered you. (Romans 6:17)

Here's my version of Romans 6:17: Instead of attempting changes you've never been able to make, feed your heart with faith righteousness! See, it works. You're not attempting anymore. Come on, stop trying to change yourself and just feed your heart with faith righteousness. The more you feed it, the less work will be involved in it. When you feed the Word of God into your spirit, you become so righteousness-conscious that sin doesn't have dominion over you. You don't pay attention to it anymore and it just goes away.

Here's what I found: the more I try to do something, the further I push it away. But if you just leave it alone and focus on God, the issue you've been dealing with will just wilt away.

Colossians 2:10 says that we are already complete in Him, so how much better can you possibly do? All you need to do is feed yourself the Word of God and just grow up in God. In the natural, you're not going to get your license until you're sixteen years of age. No matter how you bawl, squawk, and flip around on the floor, that's just the way it works.

In the kingdom of God, there are spiritual laws in place that mean you are given certain responsibilities when you reach a certain point. You're not going to get there ahead of time, praise God, but you won't get there late either.

YOU CAN'T EARN RIGHTEOUSNESS

I love Romans 7, because it shows us how Paul was trying to earn righteousness naturally. We see the dilemma where Paul says that the law is spiritual. That's so powerful. How could you ever keep a set of spiritual rules through the efforts of your flesh? It's not a natural walk, but Paul tried to walk it out naturally. People still try to live it out physically—and the result is always frustration.

That's what Paul was talking about in Philippians 3:6 when he said that he counted it all as dung. He tried keeping the law, but just keeping the law didn't profit him; he still felt guilty.

Romans 7:14 says, *"For we know that the law is spiritual..."* The law is spiritual, not natural, so how are you going to keep it by your natural self? It's an impossibility for any natural person to ever keep it. The law was never meant to be obeyed out of our flesh. Galatians 3:24 says that the law is like a schoolmaster bringing you to Christ. God never gave the law to the Israelites and then said, "Now you're going to have to keep that." He gave them all those rituals, and all those things that they'd have to do, to wear them down in their own self-righteousness. You'll never be done when you're trying to keep the law. When you realize that, you're righteous by faith like Abraham.

The Old Testament had faith just like the New Testament. When we read Hebrews 11, we find a list of people who followed God by faith, including Noah, Abel, Abraham, Isaac, and Jacob. It just goes on listing examples, the ones who operated in faith and got their names written there.

In Romans 7:14, Paul said, *"For we know that the law is spiritual: but I am carnal [a natural man], sold under sin."* Then he went on to say:

For that which I do [the Greek word katergazomai*] I allow not: for what I would, that do [*prasso*] I not; but what I hate, that do* *[poieo] I. If then I do [poieo] that which I would not, I consent unto the law that it is good. Now then it is no more I that do it, but sin that dwelleth in me.* (Romans 7:15–17)

Notice that Paul uses three different words for *do* here in these verses— *katergazomai* (something on the inside producing a wrong action), *prasso* (a practice or a habit), and *poieo* (committed to).

The Ben Campbell Johnson paraphrase says it this way:

When I experienced my contradictions so profoundly, I feel that I have no worth at all. I have the desire to perform but not the power. My lofty ideals shatter on the rocks of my actual performance. (Romans 7:18–19)[6]

And again, that's what it is—a performance. I like it when Johnson gets down to verse twenty-four, where he writes, *"Oh schizophrenic that I am…"*

I believe that the book of Romans is about Paul's Christian walk. This is how he grew in the things of the spirit of God. We see his thoughts throughout Romans 7: "God, I've spent all my life keeping the law and doing the letter of the law. I'm just a schizophrenic guy, I'm a wretched man."

If you just stop there, you wouldn't see the next verse:

I thank God through Jesus Christ our Lord. So then with the mind I myself serve the law of God; but with the flesh the law of sin. (Romans 7:25)

Paul is saying, like he said in 1 Corinthians 15:45, that his flesh came from Adam. But the next verse says that he doesn't have to listen to any negative, accusing, nagging voices anymore because he is no longer in Adam but in Christ.

---

[6] Ibid.

NO NAGGING, CONDEMNING VOICE

Romans 8 is all about being led by the Spirit. A shift has taken place here as we see that the Spirit is mentioned twenty-one times in this chapter—yet it was only mentioned once in Romans 7. Once you get past verse one— *"There is therefore now no condemnation to them which are in Christ Jesus"*—and once you stop listening to the nagging voice, you can be led by the Spirit. Being led by the Spirit simply means doing what He says. When you get free of that nagging voice and condemnation, you are free to flow with God.

According to Paul, all the law did was identify the fact that he needed a Saviour, and if he hadn't read the law he wouldn't have known that it wasn't right to covet. "Now I recognize my sin," he said. "Then I found out there is a Redeemer, somebody who could save me from my sin, somebody who could redeem my spirit, renew my mind, and save my soul." In 1 Thessalonians 5:23 Paul said, and I paraphrase, "Sanctify me wholly—spirit, soul, and body—at the rapture of the church. In my flesh dwells no good thing, but it's not a problem because this corruption will put on incorruption; this mortality will put on immortality." It's okay to fight with your flesh, which you are going to fight with until the day Jesus comes. Put it under and keep it down, but don't ever get condemned when you mess up. If you fall, just get back up.

You can just turn to Him and say, "God, I want to praise you. I thank you. Lord, I really missed it there and I repent. God, you know my heart. It wasn't my heart; it was my head, my flesh. I repent and I yield myself to you. I am powerless over this without you. I can do all things through You, but it's an impossibility to deal with this on my own. I'm not struggling with it. I'm not feeling guilty about it and I'm not coming under condemnation about it. The devil is not going to use this to eat my lunch, to beat me up. I'm not going to allow it. I'm just going to live in righteousness, peace, and joy in the Holy Ghost, and I'm still going to go out and have a good time. I'm going to laugh, because a merry heart does good like a medicine. I'm not going to allow some sickness to come into my body because I'm all fretful, worried, and condemned. I'm not ashamed of the Gospel. I serve you, God, with a pure conscience from my forefathers. They found a way to do it by faith, so we do it by faith, and now I count myself happy."

CHANGED FROM THE INSIDE-OUT

In Galatians 4:19, Paul says, "My little children, of whom I travail in birth again until Christ be formed in you…" In other words, he felt labour pains for the people of the church. Now that the Galatians were born again, his prayer was that Christ would be formed in them." The Greek word for "formed" is *morphoō*, from which we get the word metamorphosis. *Morphoō* refers to an internal change. Religion is external, but internal change comes from the Holy Spirit.

Romans 8:14 says, *"As many as are led by the Spirit of God, they are the sons of God."* If we break it down, this verse means that God wants you to hook your tongue up with your spirit, and not with your flesh or your five senses. When you hook your tongue up with the Word of God, you are led by the Spirit of God. How can you say that? Because Jesus said, in John 6:63, *"The words that I speak unto you, they are spirit, and they are life."*

You can be led by your five senses if you want to be just like the world, where men's hearts fail because of fear. Or you can stay in the Spirit and say, like the prophet Isaiah,

For, behold, the darkness shall cover the earth, and gross darkness the people: but the LORD shall arise upon thee, and his glory shall be seen upon thee. (Isaiah 60:2)

This is not a dark day for the church; the church's greatest day is upon us. We're stepping into it even now. The church that has been ridiculed for almost two thousand years is about to emerge, just like the metamorphosis of the caterpillar. You may find yourself in a place where all of a sudden you'll emerge from your cocoon and the problems—those chains that used to hold you back—just fall off you as you praise the Lord. This is the hour we are moving into right now. Let's not wait for it to come anymore; let's just embrace it. Once you receive this grace, it will set you free.

Paul said that this is an internal reality. He said, "I'm hooking my tongue up with my spirit." In other words, we shouldn't be calling things

47

the way we see them. Instead we need to be doing what Romans 4:17 says, calling those things that be not as though they were.

NOT JUST MERE MEN

Jesus told us to take His yoke upon us and learn of Him. A yoke is used to hook two oxen together, so how can two walk together unless they are agreed? (Amos 3:3) Jesus said, "If you'll hook up with Me and stop chafing your neck trying to do your own thing, if you just begin to trust in Me with all of your heart and not lean on your own way of doing things, if you'd just begin to acknowledge Me in all of your ways, then My will is to direct you."

God's will is to direct you. He desires to share every moment of the day with you and to elevate you, not to put you down. His will is to raise you up. In Ephesians 2:6, we read that He has already raised us up and seated us together in heavenly places in Christ. So why are we living like mere men?

Here's what Paul told the Corinthian Church in 1 Corinthians 3:3: "Why are you living like mere men? Why are you led by your senses?" You may be saying, "I don't have a job. I don't know what I'm going to do." Well, did you ask God for one? Put some feet to your prayers and go apply somewhere. Quit waiting for the doorbell to ring. Go apply and believe that God will open up a door. Isaiah 22:22 says that He will open up a door for you that no man can shut. God says, "I'm the one who raises up and I'm the one who puts down. I'm the one who gives promotions, so don't go to your boss—come to Me."

BOND OR FREE

Tell me, ye that desire to be under the law, do ye not hear the law? For it is written, that Abraham had two sons, the one by a bondmaid, the other by a freewoman. But he who was of the bondwoman was born after the flesh; but he of the freewoman was by promise. Which things are an allegory [or an analogy]: for these are the two covenants; the one from the mount Sinai, which gendereth to bondage... (Galatians 4:21–24).

The law was given on Mount Sinai. But what does the law do for you? What do the Ten Commandments do for you? They bring you into bondage. You will work and do your very best, and when you fail you're going to kick yourself. Then you're going to feel worse and you push even further out of your reach the thing you're trying so hard to do, because *you* are trying to do it instead of accepting it by faith.

Galatians 3:10 says that you are cursed if you try to keep the law, not if you break it. *"For as many as are of the works of the law are under the curse..."* Now let's look at this same passage in the Amplified Bible:

> *And all who depend on the Law [who are seeking to be justified by obedience to the Law of rituals] are under a curse and doomed to disappointment and destruction...* (AMP)

In other words, when you're trying to keep the law, it brings you under the curse—and the curse of the law is not poverty, sickness, and death. The curse of the law is condemnation! You feel guilt and shame. That's the reason most people who feel guilt and shame never come to church.

As the church, we're telling the world all the things they can't do, but we need to be telling them that they just need to accept Jesus and He'll work with them. Tell them that they're made in His image and His likeness and that He loves them.

SPIRIT MAN VS. THE FLESH

Galatians 4 talks about two covenants. One leads to bondage, being Hagar, a representation of the flesh. The other, being Sarah, is a representation of the Spirit.

> *For this Agar is mount Sinai in Arabia, and answereth to Jerusalem which now is, and is in bondage with her children. But Jerusalem which is above is free, which is the mother of us all.* (Galatians 4:25–26)

Then Paul goes on to quote from Isaiah 54, but what he's saying here, in modern vernacular is that Abraham, like you, was living in a tent. Your physical body is the tabernacle; it is the tent you live in. My physical body is not the real me. The real me lives inside, and inside of Abraham there were two women who had two sons. One was the law and one was grace. One was works and one was faith.

The work of the flesh produced faster, for he got Ishmael first, from the flesh. If I have these two things going on inside me, I'm trying to work the law and I've stepped out of grace. My flesh—and all of us have flesh, which we got from Adam—grows through food and development… and so does your spirit man. But my flesh is like a dog; I have to keep it on a leash. My flesh will say to me, "Why don't you have another piece of pie?" We'll just use that for an example. Your spirit man will say, "No, you ought not to do that." Now, if you are led by your flesh, you will go and have it. My spirit man has to have dominance over my flesh man.

My spirit man tells me that I am healed and made whole by the stripes of Jesus. My flesh man tells me that I'm sick, I don't feel good. If my tongue is hooked up to my spirit, my response is going to be, "By the stripes of Jesus, I am healed and made whole." If my response is, "My feet are killing me, I'm dying to go, I just feel so sick," then I'm hooked up to my flesh. That's the difference.

THE LETTER KILLS

With that in mind, we need to look at 2 Corinthians 3:6:

Who also hath made us able ministers of the new testament [this new covenant]; not of the letter [or the law], but of the spirit: for the letter [the law] killeth, but the spirit giveth life.

You need to have a revelation of this. The letter (or the law) kills, but the spirit gives life.

2 Corinthians 3:9 calls the law *"the ministry of condemnation,"* which is what the church has preached. When I got saved, I had been living a life of alcoholism and addiction. I was just so happy to be saved. I used to ride my motorcycle and sit out somewhere in God's beautiful creation

and read my Bible. While doing so, I was expecting Jesus to walk down one of those paths. I didn't feel any guilt or condemnation. I was as happy as could be...

And then I went to church and it all changed. All of a sudden there was a list of rules. The letter killed me! A year later, I was gone from the church.

Then somebody passed me some Kenneth Hagin and Kenneth Copeland tapes and brought me life. I went to my local bookstore to buy more faith material, but they had it behind the shelf in the back of the store. It was like hiding the good food while all these old snack bars were out front. You could eat all the snack bars and it would never satisfy you, but when you get into the meat of the Word of God it is fine dining!

If you're struggling with religion, I have a suggestion for you—break loose. Just break free! Receive His grace for your disgrace! But wait, we're not going to stop there. Don't tune me out now if this is making you upset. I'd either like to make you glad or make you mad, but I don't want you to stay the same as when you started reading this book.

JOSEPH—SAVIOUR OF THE WORLD

chapter four

IDENTIFY WITH BENJAMIN

I WANT TO SHOW YOU ANOTHER ANALOGY IN GENESIS, AS WE TAKE A look at the life of Joseph and his brothers. Joseph was a type of the Lord Jesus Christ in that he had a plan from God. His brothers sold him into slavery and threw him into a pit. From there, we see in Scripture how he went from the pit to the palace. It's just like how Jesus rose from hell to be seated at the Father's right hand, where He lives to make intercession for you. Well, Joseph went down to Egypt and became the saviour of the world. Just as Joseph was the saviour of the world, he had a younger brother, Benjamin, who received a blessing from the saviour of the world.

When you understand this, it will change your life forever. This message about Benjamin, and identifying yourself with him, will totally set you free, because you're going to find that he received five times as much as his brothers. Five is a representation of grace, and he received five times as much on several occasions. The thing you need to realize is that Benjamin didn't do anything to earn the blessing; all he did was receive it. There is a real lesson to be learned there in how you and I are supposed to live.

Benjamin had eleven brothers, but only he and Joseph were born of Rachel. The other ten brothers were born from Leah and Jacob's handmaids. Even though they all had the same father, they had different mothers. We will see that all of the church has one Father; one hundred percent of the church on earth has one Father, but we have different mothers, in that we're either serving God through grace or we're under the law. This will affect how you live, whether you live like a Benjamin or like one of the other brothers under the law.

TAKE AWAY THE VEIL

In looking at Genesis 29 we see that Jacob went on a journey to find his wife. When he came to the well, he encountered Rachel and fell in love with her. We also know that Moses found his wife at a well, so there is something significant about a well in the Word of God. Even Proverbs 20:5 says that wise counsel is hidden in the heart of a man and that a man of understanding will draw it out. This verse uses a well to represent the Word and wisdom of God. So when you see the well in Scripture, it's talking about a lot more than water. Wells were vital to people's lives in the Middle East; they still are today.

Jacob worked seven years for Rachel's father, Laban. The arrangement was for him to marry Rachel, but instead Laban tricked him into marrying Leah; Jacob took his bride into his tent and didn't know he had married the wrong woman until the next morning. This is why the first thing that happens in a Jewish wedding ceremony today is the groom removing the veil. It's a type of the veil that is covering the Jewish people—as well as all unsaved people—who cannot see the truth and are blinded to the things of God.

GOD WORKS IN BARREN SITUATIONS

Rachel couldn't have any children, but Leah did. Rachel was barren, and we know that God always starts with a barren situation. Whether it's Rachel or Rebecca or Sarah, it's always a barren situation. If you're in a situation that seems barren, then it's a good place for God to move. When everything seems impossible, that's when God shines. John 14:21 says that He desires to manifest Himself to you.

We know that Rachel was barren, but in Genesis 30 we see that God remembered Rachel.

And God remembered Rachel, and God hearkened to her, and opened her womb. And she conceived, and bare a son; and said, God hath taken away my reproach: and she called his name Joseph; and said, The LORD shall add to me another son. (Genesis 30:22–24)

In Genesis 35:14–18, we read,

And Jacob set up a pillar in the place where he talked with him, even a pillar of stone: and he poured a drink offering thereon, and he poured oil thereon. And Jacob called the name of the place where God spake with him, Bethel [meaning the House of God]. And they journeyed from Bethel; and there was but a little way to come to Ephrath [we understand from studying Micah and other Scripture that this is Bethlehem, the house of bread]: and Rachel travailed, and she had hard labour. And it came to pass, when she was in hard labour, that the midwife said unto her, Fear not; thou shalt have this son also. And it came to pass, as her soul was in departing, (for she died) [his birth caused her death] that she called his name Benoni [son of sorrow]: but his father called him Benjamin.

Benjamin, in the Hebrew language, means, "son of my right hand, the right hand of my righteousness, the right hand of my blessing." Before you were born again, you were a son or daughter of sorrow. Why would I say that? Isaiah 53:3 says that Jesus was a man of sorrow and acquainted with grief.

THE RIGHT HAND OF BLESSING

Genesis 48:14 will show that Joseph brought his two sons to Jacob to receive the blessing. Joseph had Ephraim on his left and Manasseh on his right, because Manasseh, the firstborn, was supposed to receive the double blessing. In the Jewish culture, the firstborn received a double portion of the inheritance, and Jacob, being related to Abraham, was a rich man. This blessing had been passed down from Abraham through Isaac and Jacob, so Manasseh was excited about receiving the blessing of the firstborn. He would get the double portion as well as the kingship, or rulership, over the household and the priesthood of the family.

At least, that's how it was supposed to happen, but what happened instead when Manasseh and his brother Ephraim were brought forward by Joseph is that the hands were switched and the blessing that was supposed to go on Manasseh went on Ephraim. Jacob reached over and crossed his hands, releasing the blessing on the younger man. Seeing what had been done, Joseph protested and said, "No, you can't do that," but the Bible says Jacob did it wittingly, or knowingly (Genesis 48:14).

Here's what was really happening. God made Jesus to be sin for us who knew no sin, in order for the gift of righteousness to be ours (2 Corinthians 5:21). The curse that was supposed to come on me went instead on Jesus and the blessing that was supposed to come on Jesus came on me. Jesus became sin for us so that we would be made the righteousness of God in Him.

So when Benjamin is called "the son of my right hand," Jacob is saying that this is the guy; this is the one who is going to receive the double blessing. If you get this by revelation, Ephesians 1:3 says that you have already been blessed with all the spiritual blessings in the heavenlies, in Christ. These spiritual blessings are received by faith. In John 14:12, Jesus said, *"Verily, verily, I say unto you, He that believeth on me, the works that I do shall he do also; and greater works than these shall he do; because I go unto my Father."* That's the double portion blessing that was spoken over the church.

JOSEPH AND JESUS

Let's look at Genesis 37 and see how Joseph is a type of Jesus, and how even Pharaoh calls him saviour of the world.

These are the generations of Jacob. Joseph, being seventeen years old, was feeding the flock with his brethren; and the lad was with the sons of Bilhah, and with the sons of Zilpah [that would have been Dan, Naphtali, Gad, and Asher, four of the twelve tribes of Israel], his father's wives: and Joseph brought unto his father their evil report. Now Israel loved Joseph more than all his children, because he was the son of his old age: and he made him a coat of many colours. (Genesis 37:2–3)

The Greek word used here for "coat of many colours" is *kuttoneth*, meaning a coat with long sleeves signifying the guy who was in charge. Have you heard the expression, "Roll up your sleeves and get to work"? Well, this guy didn't roll up his sleeves; he was the guy in charge—the boss. Everyone else had short sleeves so that they could do the work around the farm.

Genesis 37:4 says that when Joseph's brothers saw that their father loved him more than them, they hated him. In John 1:11, we also see that Jesus came unto His own, the Jewish people, and they received Him not. They rejected Jesus when He came, so you can see the type here.

EVERY KNEE WILL BOW

God gave Joseph a dream about himself, which he shared with his brothers.

And he said unto them, Hear, I pray you, this dream which I have dreamed: For, behold, we were binding sheaves in the field, and, lo, my sheaf arose, and also stood upright; and, behold, your sheaves stood round about, and made obeisance to my sheaf. (Genesis 37:6–7)

In other words, every knee would bow to him. Can you see how this is a type of the Lord Jesus?

Joseph's brothers hated him and planned to kill him. One day, they were out in a place called Dothan, feeding sheep in the desert. Joseph went looking for them at his father's request, and when they saw him coming they said, "Here comes that filthy dreamer. Let's kill him."

What did they say to Jesus? "Crucify Him! Crucify Him! Away with Him!" So it's the same type of story.

CAST INTO A PIT AND MOCKED

Come now therefore, and let us slay him, and cast him into some pit, and we will say, Some evil beast hath devoured him: and we shall see what will become of his dreams. (Genesis 37:20)

What did the Jewish people say about Jesus? "You said You can raise the temple up again in three days. Well, if You are the Son of God, come down from that cross." They mocked Him. We see the same thing happening with Joseph's brothers.

And it came to pass, when Joseph was come unto his brethren, that they stript Joseph out of his coat, his coat of many colours that was on him. (Genesis 37:23)

What did they do with Jesus? They cast lots for His garments, so again we see a type.

And they took him, and cast him into a pit: and the pit was empty, there was no water in it. (Genesis 37:24)

It was an empty, waterless well... just an empty well in the desert. When I visited Caiaphas' house during my trip to Jerusalem, in the basement of the house was a prison where criminals were held. The notable prisoners were thrown down through a hole. This hole was like an empty well, and that's where Jesus spent the night before He was crucified. The same thing happened to Joseph.

They hoisted Joseph up and sold him into slavery just as the Jews hoisted Jesus up on the cross at twelve noon as He said, "My God, My God, why have You forsaken Me?" The answer is because my sin, Gary Hooper's sin, came upon Him. All of a sudden, Jesus couldn't call God "My Father" anymore; it was "My God," because my sin came on Him and separated Him from His Father for the only time in all of history. He did that because He loves you, because He loves me.

That's exactly what's going on here with Joseph, too.

Then there passed by Midianites merchantmen; and they drew and lifted up Joseph out of the pit, and sold Joseph to the Ishmeelites for twenty pieces of silver: and they brought Joseph into Egypt. (Genesis 37:28)

How much did Judas sell Jesus for? Thirty pieces of silver, but again the same story takes place with Joseph. If we look back into Leviticus, we see what the twenty and the thirty means. Leviticus 27:3–5 speaks of the monetary value assigned to a human life at that time. Twenty pieces of silver, which Joseph was sold for, was the value placed on a male between five and twenty years of age. Thirty pieces of silver represented the price for a female slave. Jesus was betrayed for thirty pieces of silver when he redeemed us, the bride of Christ, from the slavery of sin.

DIPPED IN BLOOD

And they took Joseph's coat, and killed a kid of the goats, and dipped the coat in the blood. (Genesis 37:31)

The thing that impressed me the most about this story is that the brothers came home, threw the coat down at Jacob, and said, "Your son is dead." And he believed them. He was fooled by a bloody coat! He was walking by sight, not by faith. He accepted that truth so easily, even though it wasn't the real truth.

Revelation 19 speaks about Jesus' return, which is not so far away:

And I saw heaven opened, and behold a white horse; and he that sat upon him was called Faithful and True, and in righteousness he doth judge and make war. His eyes were as a flame of fire, and on his head were many crowns; and he had a name written, that no man knew, but he himself. And he was clothed with a vesture dipped in blood: and his name is called The Word of God. (Revelation 19:11–13)

We just read this back in Genesis, so you can see the type and the shadow again.

TWO THIEVES

In Genesis 40, we find out that Joseph was thrown into jail with two thieves. Ever wonder why there were two thieves with Jesus at the cross, one on either side? It parallels the Joseph story.

Always remember the Solomon Concept when you study the Bible. The Solomon Concept is found in Ecclesiastes 1:9—*"The thing that hath been, it is that which shall be… and there is no new thing under the sun."* History really does keep repeating itself. As a matter of fact, it will continue to repeat itself in your life unless you break the cycle. You can watch somebody work for awhile and then become unemployed, only to watch it happen all over again through the years. That's a cycle that needs to be broken. If you don't, it will just continue, over and over again until you do something different.

To break the cycle, you need to do something radical, which is what Jesus did at the cross.

PIT TO THE PALACE

I've used this expression before, saying that Joseph went from the pit to the palace, becoming an overnight success. But he spent thirteen years in the figurative pit, the longest night of his life.

In Psalm 105:19, the Bible says, "Until the time that his word came: the word of the LORD tried him." Joseph had a word from God, and he had to stand on it for thirteen years without bowing, without knuckling down. While in prison, God gave Joseph two dreams. He didn't have a Bible to read, but he had two dreams from God. God spoke to him, speaking into his heart the same way as He speaks to you and me.

God gave Joseph a word, but this verse in Psalm 105 indicates that the word took time to come to pass. That time frame was his test of faith. In other words, that trial was his trainer.

God gave him the word that carried him through great testing in the land of Egypt. Can you imagine the rejection? He was betrayed by family! How would you like to be like Joseph, who was betrayed by his whole family? How about Jesus? The Jewish people betrayed Him. The world that Jesus came to save spit in His face, whipped and beat Him, then nailed Him to a tree. So if you've been betrayed and think that nobody understands you, let me tell you that somebody does. Somebody knows what it's like to be rejected. Jesus was a man of sorrows and acquainted with grief. God did it so you could walk in His peace.

In Genesis 41, Joseph had been in prison for a couple of years when Pharaoh's men came to get him. The Bible says they came to get him hastily (Genesis 41:14) and he said no. He said, "No, I'm not going before Pharaoh until I get cleaned up." You would have thought he'd bolt out of jail, but the peace of God that surpasses understanding ruled his heart and mind. He was at peace because he was in trust. You can always tell when you're trusting God. If you're at peace, you're trusting Him, but if you're not at peace, you're not trusting Him. You can fix that by reading the Word of God and reminding yourself of who He is and whose you are. If you do, peace will come!

RULER OVER PHARAOH'S HOUSE

Thou shalt be over my house, and according unto thy word shall all my people be ruled: only in the throne will I be greater than thou. And Pharaoh said unto Joseph, See, I have set thee over all the land of Egypt. And Pharaoh took off his ring from his hand [which is like the prodigal son coming home], and put it upon Joseph's hand, and arrayed him in vestures of fine linen [just like we have been covered with a robe of righteousness and garments of salvation], and put a gold chain about his neck [which was better than a ball and chain around his ankle]; and he made him to ride in the second chariot which he had [it was second only to Pharaoh, a nice ride]; and they cried before him, Bow the knee [a type of Philippians 2:10]: and he made him ruler over all the land of Egypt. And Pharaoh said unto Joseph, I am Pharaoh, and without thee shall no man lift up his hand or foot in all the land of Egypt. And Pharaoh called Joseph's name Zaphnathpaaneah... (Genesis 41:40–45)

I like what Joseph's new name means in the Egyptian tongue: supporter of life, revealer of secrets, and saviour of the world. *"For unto you is born this day... a Saviour"* (Luke 2:11). So He is all of that: a revealer of secrets, the supporter of your life. Jesus said, *"I am come that they might have life, and that they might have it more abundantly"* (John 10:10). He came that you might experience the fullness of life, the full meal deal!

NOT RECOGNIZED

In Genesis 42, we see that there was a famine in the land. The famine lasted seven years and historians tell us that it affected the entire world. There was nothing to eat in Israel, but Jacob heard there was food in Egypt, so he sent his sons to Egypt to buy food.

It says in Genesis 42:6–7,

And Joseph was the governor over the land, and he it was that sold to all the people of the land: and Joseph's brethren came, and bowed down themselves before him with their faces to the earth [just like in the dream Joseph had]. And Joseph saw his brethren, and he knew them, but made himself strange unto them...

When Joseph saw his ten brothers, he knew who they were, but they did not recognize him—just like the Pharisees and the Sadducees didn't recognize Jesus when He came. Joseph saw an opportunity to see his brother Benjamin and explained that he would keep Simeon in custody until his brothers returned home and came back with Benjamin. Now, Benjamin was the son of Jacob's right hand and Benjamin represents you and me.

EVERYTHING IS WORKING FOR YOUR GOOD

Genesis 42:36 contains a powerful truth that we need to see:

And Jacob their father said unto them, Me have ye bereaved of my children: Joseph is not, and Simeon is not, and ye will take Benjamin away: all these things are against me.

You may think everything is stacked against you, but the truth of the matter is that everything was for Jacob and he just didn't know it. In the middle of all this, he didn't realize that everything was being provided for him. He didn't know that Pharaoh was going to say to him, "Give your father the land of Goshen, the very best of the land." He didn't understand what's written in Romans 8:28, *"that all things work together for good to them that love God, to them who are called according to his purpose."* He didn't understand that; he was in a mess, and therefore he was anxious.

Be careful [anxious] for nothing; but in every thing by prayer and supplication with thanksgiving let your requests be made known unto God. (Philippians 4:6)

Let the peace of God rule in your hearts... and be ye thankful. (Colossians 3:15)

Why are you thankful? Because you know that He heard you. 1 John 5:13–14 says that if you know He heard you, you also know that the petition you brought to Him is granted unto you.

We've now established that Joseph is a type of Jesus. Joseph was a saviour in the world and we can say that Jesus is our Joseph in heaven.

GRACE AND PEACE TO YOU

And when Joseph came home, they brought him the present which was in their hand into the house, and bowed themselves to him to the earth. And he asked them of their welfare, and said, Is your father well, the old man of whom ye spake? Is he yet alive? And they answered, Thy servant our father is in good health, he is yet alive. And they bowed down their heads, and made obeisance. And he lifted up his eyes, and saw his brother Benjamin, his mother's son, and said, Is this your younger brother, of whom ye spake unto me? And he said, God be gracious unto thee, my son. (Genesis 43:26–29)

If you want to see how God looks at you, you can see it here. Look at the very first words that Joseph speaks to Benjamin, the same words that God speaks to you: *"God be gracious unto thee, my son."* In other words, "Grace and peace be unto you." In Paul's letters, we see that he always greets his readers by saying, *"Grace and peace be multiplied unto you through the knowledge of God… that hath called us to glory and virtue"* (2 Peter 1:2–3). In his pastoral letters, the books of 1 and 2 Timothy and Titus, Paul writes: *"Grace, mercy, and peace be unto you."* This is the way God addresses people. Oh Daniel, my beloved! Oh Gary, my beloved! Oh Tom, my beloved! Oh Nancy, my beloved! This is how God speaks to us. Grace and peace be unto you!

And Joseph made haste; for his bowels did yearn upon his brother [remember, God's grace abounds toward you]: and he sought where to weep; and he entered into his chamber, and wept there. And he washed his face, and went out, and refrained himself, and said, Set on bread. And they set on for him by himself, and for them by themselves, and for the Egyptians, which did eat with him, by themselves: because the Egyptians might not eat bread with the Hebrews; for that is an abomination unto the Egyptians. And they sat before him, the firstborn according to his birthright, and the youngest according to his youth: and the men marvelled one at another. And he took and sent messes unto them from before him: but Benjamin's mess was five times so much as any of theirs. And they drank, and were merry with him. (Genesis 43:30–34)

God will prepare a table for you even in the presence of your enemies (Psalm 23), and you can expect five times as much from Him if you are Benjamin. Joseph wept when he saw Benjamin, whom he loved most since they had the same mother, giving them a special bond.

WE ALL HAVE THE SAME FATHER

Remember, all Christians have the same Father but different mothers. What do I mean by that? Leah represents worry and anxiety (religion), whereas Rachel represents grace. If you are under the law, Galatians 3:17–19 says that you're still living under the curse even though Galatians 3:13 says that Christ has redeemed us from the curse of the law. Christ was made a curse for us, for it is written that cursed is the one who hangs on the tree. Why was He cursed? So that the blessing could come upon you and me (Galatians 3:14). You and I are supposed to be walking in the blessing of Abraham, a blessing which came upon the Gentiles. We're supposed to have the blessing in operation in our lives, but if we're under the law, then we feel guilty and condemned and we don't believe that God wants to prosper us.

We may even be dealing with sickness and disease. I once heard a doctor say that ninety percent of all diseases are caused from having a bad thought life. The diseases people find themselves with don't come from eating too much fried food. I know there are things you should and shouldn't eat, as far as energy and nutrition go; I don't want to put regular gasoline in my high-test motorcycle, because it won't work the same. I understand that, but I also understand that the wages of sin is death and that anything that's not of faith is sin. So, when I'm living in anxiety or when I'm living in condemnation, I promote these chemicals being released from my brain that confuse my body and bring sickness and disease!

Look at what Joseph says to Benjamin: "God be gracious unto you, my son." Gracious here means to bend, to stoop down in kindness. It means to bestow a blessing upon someone. We see that Benjamin received five times more than his other brothers. Now that's blessing!

In Genesis 45, we read that Jacob was expecting the worst, but look at the promise that is here for him.

And Pharaoh said unto Joseph, Say unto thy brethren, This do ye; lade your beasts, and go, get you unto the land of Canaan; and take your father and your households, and come unto me: and I will give you the good of the land of Egypt, and ye shall eat the fat of the land. Now thou art commanded, this do ye; take you wagons out of the land of Egypt for your little ones, and for your wives, and bring your father, and come. Also regard not your stuff; for the good of all the land of Egypt is yours. (Genesis 45:17–20, emphasis added)

That's what God is showing you and me in His Word. All the good of the land is ours. When we walk free from condemnation and keep our eyes on God's promise, we too will walk in the fullness of that blessing!

BENJAMIN—SON OF HIS RIGHT HAND

---
chapter five

IN THE PREVIOUS CHAPTER, WE EXPLORED THE ANALOGY THAT YOU ARE Benjamin. Let's establish that idea some more by looking at Genesis 35.

> And God appeared unto Jacob again, when he came out of Padanaram, and blessed him. And God said unto him, Thy name is Jacob: thy name shall not be called any more Jacob, but Israel shall be thy name: and he called his name Israel. And God said unto him, I am God Almighty [or El Shaddai]: be fruitful and multiply [just as He told Adam and Eve]; a nation [that's the Jews] and a company of nations [that's the Gentiles] shall be of thee [shall come out of you], and kings shall come out of thy loins; and the land which I gave Abraham and Isaac, to thee I will give it [Galatians 3:29 says that Abraham's seed is heir to the same promise], and to

thy seed after thee [that's us] will I give the land. And God went up
from him in the place where he talked with him. And Jacob set up a
pillar in the place where he talked with him, even a pillar of stone:
and he poured a drink offering thereon, and he poured oil thereon.
And Jacob called the name of the place where God spake with him,
Bethel [house of God]. And they journeyed from Bethel; and there
was but a little way to come to Ephrath [Bethlehem, where Jesus
was born]: and Rachel travailed, and she had hard labour. And
it came to pass, when she was in hard labour, that the midwife
said unto her, Fear not; thou shalt have this son also. And it came
to pass, as her soul was in departing, (for she died) that she called
his name Benoni: but his father called him Benjamin. (Genesis
35:9–18)

Rachel had to die in order for Benjamin to live. This is very
significant, because someone had to die for you to live as well. We also
see in this passage that she called him Benoni, which means "son of
sorrow," but Israel called him Benjamin, which is "son of the right hand."
We understand from Isaiah 53:3 that Jesus was a man of sorrow and
acquainted with grief. We also talked about the changing of the hands
when Joseph brought Ephraim and Manasseh to receive the blessing,
and how the blessing went on Ephraim.

We have seen how Joseph was taken from the pit to the palace
overnight—well, it was thirteen years coming, but when it happened it
was overnight. I don't know how long you have been walking things out
with God and waiting to see some situation in your life turn around, but
don't ever get discouraged. As long as you're breathing, even if only one
nostril is out of the water, make sure you're declaring, "Jesus is Lord!" If
you don't quit, you'll see the goodness of God in your life.

Can you imagine being in the lowest part of the country, in the
prison, and then the very next day you're in the palace? God can make
sudden changes in your life. You can be going one way, full steam ahead,
then suddenly find yourself going in another direction.

A lot of Christians don't even know what they have been called for.
So, the first thing you and I need to know is why we were designed and

what the designer had in mind for each of us. If you don't establish that, you'll never know where you're going, but if you get that established and set it in front of you, then it doesn't matter what's going on. When you know what your destination is, there may be obstacles to manoeuvre around, but you'll still have your focus. Joseph didn't have the Bible, but he had two dreams from God, one for himself and another for the nation of Israel, so he knew where he was going.

If you don't know where you're going, how will you ever know when you get there? Joseph knew his purpose. He was so calm when the guards came to get him out of jail that even Paul the Apostle, being from the tribe of Benjamin, learned something from it. Paul understood grace, and in Acts 16, when he was thrown into jail, Paul remembered Joseph's story. His mind went back to what Joseph did, and then he decided to operate the same way.

SAVIOUR OF THE WORLD

We found in the previous chapter that Joseph was the saviour of the world. In the Egyptian tongue, his new name meant *"the supporter of life, the revealer of secrets"* (Genesis 41:45). Joseph was called the saviour of the world just like Jesus is the Saviour of the world. Jesus is now in heaven, whereas Joseph was operating on the earth. Whenever you read about Joseph, think about Jesus.

Psalm 105:17 says, *"He sent a man before them, even Joseph, who was sold for a servant."*

What does it say in Philippians 2?

Who, being in the form of God [talking about Jesus], thought it not robbery to be equal with God: but made himself of no reputation, and took upon him the form of a servant, *and was made in the likeness of men: and being found in fashion as a man, he humbled himself, and became obedient unto death, even the death of the cross.* (Philippians 2:6–8)

Then, in Mark 10:45, Jesus said,

For even the Son of man came not to be ministered unto, but to minister, and to give his life a ransom for many. (Mark 10:45)

Let's continue reading from Psalm 105:

He sent a man before them, even Joseph, who was sold for a servant: whose feet they hurt with fetters: he was laid in iron: until the time that his word came: the word of the LORD tried him. (Psalm 105:17–19)

Just as Abraham was tried in Genesis 22 when he offered up his son Isaac.

How can Abraham do that? Jesus said, *"Abraham rejoiced to see my day: and he saw it, and was glad"* (John 8:56). When Abraham began to rejoice to God, God showed him the future. Before Abraham ever offered up Isaac, he knew that Jesus was going to take Isaac's place. That's why Abraham was convinced and fully persuaded. You cannot be fully persuaded unless you have a word from God.

YOUR TRIAL IS YOUR TRAINER

It's not a surprise to see in Psalm 105:19 that Joseph was tried. In Luke 22:31–32, Jesus said to Simon Peter,

Simon, Simon, behold, Satan hath desired to have you, that he may sift you as wheat: but I have prayed for thee, that thy faith fail not...

So we know that Peter was going to be tried. When you look up the word "tried," it means to smelt, to refine, to separate the precious from the natural. Peter said that the trying of one's faith is more precious than gold, which perishes (1 Peter 1:7). A blacksmith would keep working a piece of gold until he had removed all the dross, until he could see his face reflected in the gold. In the same way, you are like pressurized wood. You are being pressure-treated so that you can withstand every storm of life.

If there's no pressure on you, something's wrong. We are trained to think that something is wrong when we have pressure on us, but no, it's the other way around. You can't build a deck out of regular wood, because it will rot and fade away, so you buy pressure-treated wood because it lasts longer. So, the word "tried" also means to polish, to make elegant, to improve accuracy.

So we could say it this way: your trial is your trainer. If you try to jump the process in the name of progress, and lots of people do, you jump out of the process. Don't try to escape it! In Psalm 23:4, David said, *"Yea, though I walk through the valley..."* (emphasis mine). He didn't say "though I *escape* the valley." There was no escape for him; the only way out was through.

Lots of times people find themselves in bad marriage situations and think that divorce is the answer. I have a friend who's been divorced four times because he kept marrying the wrong woman. Guess what? It wasn't the wrong woman. You can figure it out after a while—the problem was the guy.

We try to get out of the pressure of personal change. We think that if we can change something externally, if we can just change people or situations on the outside, then everything will be fine. No. Until you change yourself, nothing out there will change. When I was in Narcotics Anonymous, we called this the geographical change. If I could just live in a different city, maybe everything would be better. No. The problem with that is that I would still be there. So that doesn't work. The change needs to take place on the inside.

WHOSE HOUSE ARE WE?

Joseph had to go through all of this. There was no escaping this time in his life. If we read on, we find out that he was sent to Egypt on purpose. Psalm 105:17 tells us that God sent two men before the Hebrew nation—one being Joseph and the other being Yeshua Ben David, Jesus the Son of God, the son of David.

Until the time that his word came: the word of the LORD tried him [speaking about Joseph]. The king sent and loosed him; even the ruler of the people, and let him go free. He made him lord of his house, and ruler of all his substance. (Psalm 105:19–21)

Hebrews 3:6 says that Jesus is the Lord over this house, whose house are we:

But Christ as a son over his own house; whose house are we, if we hold fast the confidence and the rejoicing of the hope firm unto the end.

Hebrews 1:9 says that because He went through all the testing and pressure, He was anointed with the oil of gladness above His fellows. In other words, because He passed the test, He was overflowing with joy, and for the joy that was set before Him, He endured the cross and the shame of it (Hebrews 12:2).

Joseph went through some things because there was joy on the other side. There's always joy in doing God's will. Going through the process is no fun. Faith isn't fun, but telling the story afterwards is fun. I love faith, but I don't enjoy it. I don't enjoy walking by what I can't see until I can see it. It's easier the other way, but that's false progress; that's Ishmael instead of Isaac. Pharaoh made Joseph lord over all his house and ruler over all of his substance, to bind princes at his pleasure, and to teach senators wisdom (Genesis 41). Joseph became the top guy in the whole country.

For every house is builded by some man; but he that built all things is God. And Moses verily was faithful in all his house, as a servant, for a testimony of those things which were to be spoken after; but Christ as a son over his own house; whose house are we, if we hold fast the confidence and the rejoicing of the hope firm unto the end. (Hebrews 3:4–6)

This is just like Psalm 105. Christ was faithful as a servant in the same way that Joseph was faithful as a servant. When bad things happen and you *know* God, not when you know *about* God, you will still trust

Him. You won't necessarily understand everything, but you'll say, "Hey, I don't understand this, but I know You, Jesus. I know that You will never leave me, You will never fail me, and You will never forsake me, so I'm at peace. I'm at peace in the middle of the storm and I'm at peace in the middle of turmoil."

BREAD IN THE LAND OF EGYPT

In Genesis 42, Jacob saw that there was bread, or wheat, in Egypt.

Now when Jacob saw that there was corn in Egypt, Jacob said unto his sons, Why do ye look one upon another? (Genesis 42:1)

This sounds just like the lepers in 2 Kings 7:4, who said, "Why should we sit here until we die?" That's the way a lot of Christians live: "If I can just make it to the grave without any trouble…" No, don't just survive—thrive!

And he said, Behold, I have heard that there is corn in Egypt: get you down thither, and buy for us from thence; that we may live, and not die. And Joseph's ten brethren went down to buy corn in Egypt. But Benjamin [meaning "son of my right hand"], Joseph's brother, Jacob sent not with his brethren; for he said, Lest peradventure mischief befall him. And the sons of Israel came to buy corn among those that came: for the famine was in the land of Canaan. And Joseph was the governor over the land, and he it was that sold to all the people of the land: and Joseph's brethren came, and bowed down themselves before him with their faces to the earth. (Genesis 42:2–6)

They didn't recognize Joseph, but they were fulfilling prophecy, because they didn't recognize him the first time, just like Jesus wasn't recognized by the Jews the first time He came. It's not until Zechariah 12:10 that the Bible says they'll look upon Him whom they have pierced, the One that they sold into slavery.

See, the story is exactly the same. The Jews said about Jesus, "Get Him out of here. Get this dreamer away from us." Joseph's brothers said the same thing: "Get this guy away from us. He's messing us up. We have our own deal going on and here comes that dreamer. Let's get rid of him." Let's get rid of Jesus, let's get rid of Joseph: same story.

And Joseph saw his brethren, and he knew them, but made himself strange unto them, and spake roughly unto them; and he said unto them, Whence come ye? And they said, From the land of Canaan to buy food. And Joseph knew his brethren, but they knew not him. And Joseph remembered the dreams which he dreamed of them, and said unto them, Ye are spies; to see the nakedness of the land ye are come. And they said unto him, Nay, my lord, but to buy food are thy servants come. We are all one man's sons; we are true men, thy servants are no spies. And he said unto them, Nay, but to see the nakedness of the land ye are come. And they said, Thy servants are twelve brethren, the sons of one man in the land of Canaan; and, behold, the youngest is this day with our father, and one is not. And Joseph said unto them, That is it that I spake unto you, saying, Ye are spies: Hereby ye shall be proved: By the life of Pharaoh ye shall not go forth hence, except your youngest brother come hither. Send one of you, and let him fetch your brother, and ye shall be kept in prison, that your words may be proved, whether there be any truth in you: or else by the life of Pharaoh surely ye are spies. (Genesis 42:7–16)

See, the first time the brothers came, they were in bondage. Verse seventeen says, *"And he put them all together into ward three days."* Anytime you see a reference to three days, you can look for a redeemer on the fourth day.

And Joseph said unto them the third day, This do, and live; for I fear God: if ye be true men, let one of your brethren be bound in the house of your prison: go ye, carry corn for the famine of your houses: but bring your youngest brother unto me; so shall your words be verified, and ye shall not die. And they did so. And they said one to another, We are verily guilty concerning our brother, in that we saw the anguish of his soul, when he besought us, and we would not hear; therefore is this distress come upon us [so it turns out that they knew]. And Reuben answered them, saying, Spake I not unto you, saying, Do not sin against the child; and ye would not hear? therefore, behold, also his blood is required. And they knew not that Joseph understood them; for he spake unto them by an interpreter. (Genesis 42:18–23)

The Jews didn't understand Jesus, either. The disciples said, "Why do you speak to them in parables? You tell us plainly, but You speak to the crowd in parables."

And he turned himself about from them, and wept; and returned to them again, and communed with them, and took from them Simeon, and bound him before their eyes. (Genesis 42:24)

If you're wondering why Joseph picked Simeon, one thing that comes to mind is that Simeon's name comes from the word *shammah*, which means "to hear." Researching this word led me to Luke 2, so let's take a look at the first Jew to get born again.

And, behold, there was a man in Jerusalem, whose name was Simeon; and the same man was just and devout, waiting for the consolation of Israel [just as Simeon, Joseph's step-brother, was doing down in Egypt when his brothers left to get Benjamin]: and the Holy Ghost was upon him. And it was revealed unto him by the Holy Ghost, that he should not see death, before he had seen the Lord's Christ. And he came by the Spirit into the temple: and when the parents brought in the child Jesus, to do for him after the custom of the law [to be circumcised], then took he him up in his arms, and blessed God, and said, Lord, now lettest thou thy servant depart in peace, according to thy word: for mine eyes have seen thy salvation. (Luke 2:25–30)

The word "behold" is like saying, "Hey, look and see! I've got something here, some heavy revelation. I have some holy information being laid out here."

GRACE BRINGS BLESSING

Then Joseph commanded to fill their sacks with corn, and to restore every man's money into his sack, and to give them provision for the way: and thus did he unto them. And they laded their asses with the corn, and departed thence. And as one of them opened his sack to give his ass provender in the inn, he espied his money; for, behold, it was in his sack's mouth [the asses were carrying bags of wheat]. And he said unto his brethren, My money is restored... (Genesis 42:25–28)

The Jewish nation today is blessed, but it doesn't even know why. The reason Hitler wanted to kill them all was because it didn't matter where you put them; they would prosper and end up owning all the banks. Over my years, I've watched this trend continue with banks, the movie industry, and big celebrities. The Jews I personally know have always walked in the blessing, whether they knew why it was or not.

And he said unto his brethren, My money is restored; and, lo, it is even in my sack: and their heart failed them, and they were afraid, saying one to another, What is this that God hath done unto us? (Genesis 42:28)

As we continue in Genesis 42, we see that Joseph's brothers returned home and told Jacob, "We have to send Benjamin down there or we can't go back and get Simeon." It's amazing to me that they didn't bother thinking about Simeon again until after the food ran out. Did you ever notice that? It's not like they said, "Let's get back there right away and get Simeon." It didn't happen until they were hungry.

And Jacob their father said unto them, Me have ye bereaved of my children: Joseph is not, and Simeon is not, and ye will take Benjamin away: all these things are against me. (Genesis 42:36, emphasis mine)

That last line is a powerful thing to underline in your Bible, because it shows that Jacob was walking by sight, believing everything was against him. However, in the Spirit, everything was working *for* him because Pharaoh was prepared to give him the land of Goshen. Pharaoh had told Joseph to bring his family down and give them the best that the world had to offer. See, this is exactly what God would say to us today: "I want to give you the best that the world has to offer. I'm not out to get you."

Consider the woman caught in adultery in John 8. Adultery is a serious matter, yet we see that the first words Jesus said to the woman after the crowd left were, *"Neither do I condemn thee"* (John 8:11). His words are amazing to me. Just a half-hour earlier, maybe an hour earlier, she was in bed with someone else's husband and now she knelt at the feet of Jesus. All the religious crowd was saying, "Stone her to death," but Jesus said, "Hey, I don't condemn you. And because you're not condemned, you can go and sin no more."

He didn't come to condemn the world, but to reconcile the world (John 3:17). Religious people got so mad when He said that, and I understand why. They were working so hard trying to please God! Then a woman came along who was caught in the act of adultery, but Jesus just forgave her and freed her from condemnation. Religion would say, "What do you mean, you forgive her? Well, surely she's got to do some kind of penance. Oh yes, you forgive her, but she's not going to serve in any place of ministry, I'll tell you that right now. She's not going to be allowed to do anything around here, at least not for a couple of years." Is that right? How can a person say that without condemnation? When you receive true forgiveness, you are restored. That messes up religion, but that's the simplicity of Christ.

Paul said that we shouldn't let anybody pull us away from the simplicity that's in Christ (2 Corinthians 11:3). You might say, "You mean to tell me that we have a license to sin?" No, that's a license to live right! Knowing that God loves me that much makes me never want to do anything wrong. I'll want to do everything right. I don't *have* to; I just *want* to. It's better that way. When you *have to do it*, you just keep pushing it further away and keep failing at it. When you just *want to*, it becomes easy because it comes from a heart relationship, not just head knowledge.

Jacob believed that everything was against him, but that wasn't true. When we get into Genesis 45, you see the blessing God had lined up for them in Egypt.

And the famine was sore in the land. And it came to pass, when they had eaten up the corn which they had brought out of Egypt, their father said unto them, Go again, buy us a little food. (Genesis 43:1–2)

Notice that Jacob didn't even say, "Go get Simeon." He said, "Go get something to eat."

If thou wilt send our brother with us, we will go down and buy thee food: but if thou wilt not send him, we will not go down: for the man said unto us, Ye shall not see my face, except your brother be with you. (Genesis 43:4–5)

And when Joseph saw Benjamin with them [or when Jesus sees you], he said to the ruler of his house, Bring these men home, and slay, and make ready [this is a type of the prodigal story, with the killing of the fatted calf in Luke 15:11]; for these men shall dine with me at noon. (Genesis 43:16)

The first time the brothers came, they were put in jail for three days, just like the law brings all believers into bondage. What does grace bring us into? It brings us over to the house, just like Hebrews 3:6 says— *"Whose house are we?"* The second time the brothers came, they were brought into Joseph's house.

And the man did as Joseph bade; and the man brought the men into Joseph's house. And the men were afraid, because they were brought into Joseph's house; and they said, Because of the money that was returned in our sacks at the first time are we brought in; that he may seek occasion against us, and fall upon us, and take us for bondmen, and our asses. (Genesis 43:17–18)

Let's continue reading from Genesis 43.

And when Joseph came home, they brought him the present which was in their hand into the house, and bowed themselves to him to the earth. And he asked them of their welfare, and said, Is your father well, the old man of whom ye spake? Is he yet alive? And they answered, Thy servant our father is in good health, he is yet alive. And they bowed down their heads, and made obeisance. And he lifted up his eyes, and saw his brother Benjamin [Jesus is the first born among many brethren], his mother's son, and said, Is this your younger brother, of whom ye spake unto me? And he said, God be gracious unto thee, my son. (Genesis 43: 26–29)

This is exactly what Jesus would do if He were to appear and look at you right now. He'd say, *"Grace and peace be multiplied unto you through the knowledge of God... that hath called us to glory and virtue"* (2 Peter 1:2–3).

And Joseph made haste; for his bowels did yearn upon his brother: and he sought where to weep; and he entered into his chamber, and wept there. (Genesis 43:30)

God's grace abounds towards you, just like Joseph's yearning for his brother, to do something for you, to do something in your life. The only thing that's stopping Him is that we don't have the faith to realize we are like Benjamin, the son of God's right hand. Instead we think we're one of the other brothers. They all had the same father, but they had different mothers: one was under the law and the other was under grace. If you're living under the law, you're obeying the Ten Commandments to the best of your ability. Then your worth is based on the best of *your* ability, but if you live by grace, it has nothing to do with your ability. Without faith it is impossible to please God, but if you can learn how to live by faith and not by works, you'll live according to what has already been done. You will live a Benjamin life.

Benjamin didn't deserve any of this blessing. He couldn't have earned any of it, but it came to him because he was family and Joseph loved him the most. Make sure you're under grace and not under the law. If you do, God will love you the most.

Continuing in Genesis 43, we read,

> *And they sat before him, the firstborn according to his birthright, and the youngest according to his youth: and the men marveled one at another.* (Genesis 43:33)

They marvelled at Joseph's ability to arrange them by age, because they still didn't know who Joseph was. He sat Rueben on one side and Benjamin on the other, just like at the Last Supper; Judas, the oldest, was on one side and John, the youngest, was on the other side of Jesus.

> *And he took and sent messes unto them from before him: but Benjamin's mess was five times so much as any of theirs. And they drank, and were merry with him.* (Genesis 43:34)

They all drank and were merry. They all partook of the feast, but the one who was living by faith and under grace (Benjamin) received five times as much.

THE NUMBER OF GRACE

The number five is the number for *grace*, and the fifth letter of the Hebrew alphabet is the type of the Holy Spirit. Anytime you find the number *five* in Scripture, you will find *grace* hooked up to it. How many stones did David pick up when he was going to kill Goliath? Five. It was God's grace that killed Goliath, because you can't throw a stone hard enough to sink through someone's skull when you hit him in the forehead, can you? No, that thing was jet-propelled. Grace did it. Grace defeated the enemy.

> *And he commanded the steward of his house, saying, Fill the men's sacks with food, as much as they can carry, and put every man's money in his sack's mouth. And put my cup, the silver cup, in the sack's mouth of the youngest.* (Genesis 44:1)

Hallelujah! In Leviticus 5, we see that silver represents redemption, making this the silver cup of redemption on top of the wheat. Redemption will be on top of the harvest of souls in this last day. The people who are preaching grace are going to experience a huge harvest. When people are caught in adultery, they will experience forgiveness. When unmarried people are living together, nobody will say, "Well, you better just stop that." No. When you hang around Jesus and His anointing, all that will stop. You don't have to address it! You don't have to be the Pharisee police or the temple cops; we don't need those in the kingdom of God.

This is why the church hasn't grown. We have too many Pharisees, too many people who can quote the Word but don't show love. Without love, the Bible can be hard on you. If you don't understand the grace of God, you can read His Word and get all bummed out. Have you ever received an email from somebody and wondered what their mood was? That's what I don't like about written communication; sometimes it's hard to tell if the person is laughing or if they're mad at you. You don't hear it the way they said it; you hear it the way you think they said it. It's like you don't see things the way they are. You see things the way *you* are. So if you look at the Bible and you're filled with rejection, you don't see grace. Instead you just see a God who's ticked off at you.

And put my cup, the silver cup, in the sack's mouth of the youngest, and his corn money. And he did according to the word that Joseph had spoken. (Genesis 44:2)

The wheat doesn't just represent the harvest. Think of the wheat, or bread, as the Word of God. We can say it this way, "On top of the Word of God, you have to have grace." You have to have redemption power, or all you're left with is the law, which is powerless and cold and will hurt people.

Then Joseph could not refrain himself before all them that stood by him; and he cried, Cause every man to go out from me. And there stood no man with him, while Joseph made himself known unto his brethren. And he wept aloud: and the Egyptians and the house

of Pharaoh heard. And Joseph said unto his brethren, I am Joseph; doth my father yet live? And his brethren could not answer him; for they were troubled at his presence. And Joseph said unto his brethren, Come near to me, I pray you. And they came near. And he said, I am Joseph your brother, whom ye sold into Egypt. Now therefore be not grieved, nor angry with yourselves, that ye sold me hither: for God did send me before you to preserve life. For these two years hath the famine been in the land: and yet there are five years, in which there shall neither be eating nor harvest. And God sent me before you to preserve you a posterity in the earth, and to save your lives by a great deliverance. So now it was not you that sent me hither, but God: and he hath made me a father to Pharaoh, and lord of all his house, and a ruler throughout all the land of Egypt.
(Genesis 45:1–8)

We can say, in our day, "Jesus is Lord of all!" Isaiah 53:10 says just what Joseph said here, *"It pleased the LORD to bruise him."* In other words, "You thought that you did it, but God did it to me. God did this." What Joseph was saying to his brothers was similar to Romans 8:1. Essentially, he said, "Don't be condemned, my brothers, because it wasn't you who did this. My Father sent me here."

PROVISIONS FOR THE JOURNEY HOME

Let's continue reading at Genesis 45:13.

And ye shall tell my father of all my glory in Egypt [in the world], and of all that ye have seen; and ye shall haste and bring down my father hither. And he fell upon his brother Benjamin's neck, and wept; and Benjamin wept upon his neck. Moreover he kissed all his brethren, and wept upon them: and after that his brethren talked with him. And the fame thereof was heard in Pharaoh's house, saying, Joseph's brethren are come: and it pleased Pharaoh well, and his servants. And Pharaoh said unto Joseph, Say unto thy brethren, This do ye; lade your beasts, and go, get you unto the land of Canaan; and take your father and your households, and come unto me: and I will give you the good of the land of Egypt [of the world], and ye shall eat the fat of the land. Now thou art commanded, this do ye; take you wagons out of the land of Egypt for your little ones, and for your wives, and bring your father, and come. Also regard not your stuff; for the good of all the land of Egypt is yours [you don't have to fuss about your stuff; everything is yours, the earth is yours]. And the children of Israel did so: and Joseph gave them wagons, according to the commandment of Pharaoh, and gave them provision for the way. To all of them he gave each man changes of raiment [Jesus, too, clothed you with garments of salvation and covered you with a robe of righteousness]; but to Benjamin he gave three hundred pieces of silver, and five changes of raiment [again, the grace people get five times as much]. And to his father he sent after this manner; ten asses laden with the good things of Egypt [all of the world's goods], and ten she asses laden with corn and bread and meat for his father by the way. So he sent his brethren away, and they departed: and he said unto them, See that ye fall not out by the way. (Genesis 45:13–24)

We know from study of the Hebrew language that the ten days from Rosh Hashanah to Yom Kippur are ten days of judgement. We see these ten asses laden with corn and bread signifying that grace overrides judgement.

All of these provisions were for the journey home. *"Forget not all his benefits"* (Psalm 103:2). He'll daily load you with benefits. So, Joseph sent his brothers away and they departed. Now, look what happens when they get back.

And they went up out of Egypt, and came into the land of Canaan [the promised land] unto Jacob their father, and told him, saying, Joseph is yet alive, and he is governor over all the land of Egypt. And Jacob's heart fainted, for he believed them not [as an unbeliever, he is known as Jacob; as a believer, he is known as Israel]. And they told him all the words of Joseph, which he had said unto them: and when he saw the wagons which Joseph had sent to carry him, the spirit of Jacob their father revived. (Genesis 45:25–27)

Do you want revival? Jacob saw, and then he believed. The world has to see to believe. Even John the beloved, when he ran into the empty tomb, saw that the body was gone before he believed. We can't just tell the world how good our God is. They won't believe it. But if they see it, they will believe. The word "revive," in the Hebrew, is *chayah*, which can mean born again, or revival. In Genesis 46:1, Jacob's name is changed back to Israel. That's because he didn't believe what he heard. Once he believed, he goes back to being called Israel again.

God's Word just keeps unfolding the more we dig into it. When I imagine heaven, I see a big Bible study with people sitting around in no hurry to go anywhere. A million years from now, we'll still be learning new things. I've been studying God's Word for thirty years and every single day I find something that I didn't see before. It's just like the angels around the throne of God for all of eternity. Every time they look upon the face of Jesus, they cry out, "Holy, Holy, Holy is the Lord God Almighty," because each time they see Him they see something new and different. This earth will seem very dim and boring after you've been to heaven.

ACTIONS SPEAK LOUDER

As we wrap up, let's look in Ecclesiastes 9.

Now there was found in it [a city] a poor wise man, and he by his wisdom delivered the city; yet no man remembered that same poor man [because he had no influence]. Then said I, Wisdom is better than strength: nevertheless the poor man's wisdom is despised [not respected], and his words are not heard [not heeded]. (Ecclesiastes 9:15–16)

As long as I can remember, all the churches I've ever been in (except my current one) say things like, "Let's go set up a soup kitchen. Let's go meet the needs of the poor." Now, that's a good thing. The Bible commands us to do that, so don't think I'm diminishing it at all. But there's a whole group of people who no one has ever reached—we call them the "up and outers." Poor people think that if they had a little bit of money, things would be perfect, whereas many wealthy people have the money and realize it isn't the answer. We could say to these wealth people, "God is good," and they'll say, "You're behind in your rent…" They look at our behaviours and actions and think, "If God is good, where is His goodness?" So, our actions have to change for us to effectively preach the Gospel, and they will change when we get a revelation of the fact that we are like Benjamin.

You don't have to position yourself as being holy to get God to move on your behalf. No. First you believe, and then you receive! You just have to realize that God looks at you the same way Joseph looked at and yearned for Benjamin. God yearns for you. He's impassioned by you! Read James 4, and see that He boils over with jealousy for you. The more time you give Him, the more time He will want, because He wants to spend every moment of every day with you!

THE RIGHT HAND OF GOD

---

chapter six

WE'VE LOOKED AT THE LIVES OF JOSEPH AND HIS YOUNGER BROTHER, Benjamin. Jesus was the firstborn among many brethren, but Benjamin was Joseph's only younger brother. He had many older brothers, who sold Joseph into slavery, but only Benjamin and Joseph shared the same mother.

We saw that Joseph was thrown into a pit and left there for a while, just like Jesus languished overnight in the pit at Caiaphas' basement before His execution. Joseph was brought out of the pit and sold into slavery and sent down to Egypt. Jesus was also sold into slavery—the slavery of our sin. Joseph was in Egypt thirteen years and began his ministry at age thirty, the same age at which Jesus began His ministry.

There is another symbolic parallel to observe in Genesis 22, where Abraham offered up Isaac. Abraham looked behind him and saw a ram caught in the thicket by his horns. Thousands of years later, Jesus had a crown of thorns pressed down upon Him, the thorns representing our sin.

When Joseph was in Egypt, he was even thrown into jail with two thieves, just like Jesus was crucified between two thieves. One thief at the cross was saved and the other wasn't. We see the same thing with Joseph—one thief, the cupbearer, was spared his life, and the other, the baker, was executed.

Joseph had a coat with long sleeves. Your Bible might say "many colours," but the Hebrew word is *kuttoneth*, meaning long sleeves; the man in charge had the long-sleeved coat whereas everyone under him had their sleeves rolled up for work. This tells us that Joseph was placed "in charge" over his brothers. His brothers didn't like him. They said he was a dreamer and they wanted to kill him. When Jesus came, his fellow Jews didn't like Him either—and He was called a dreamer, too. The Jews wanted to kill Him, crying, "Crucify Him! Crucify Him!"

Joseph rose from the prison and Jesus rose from the grave. When Pharaoh called Joseph up out of prison to interpret his dreams, Pharaoh told him that he would be second in the kingdom, just like Jesus is second in the kingdom of God. At that time, Pharaoh changed Joseph's name to mean "saviour of the world" (we understand that Egypt is a type of the world). As Joseph became in charge of all Egypt, his brothers came down because there was a famine in the land and they needed food, which Egypt had in ample supply. When they got there, they didn't recognize him. We know that when Jesus came, the Jews didn't recognize Him, either.

Zechariah 12:10 says that when He comes back again, the people will look upon Him whom they have pierced. When Joseph's brothers came, he didn't reveal himself until Benjamin was brought to him—and Benjamin represents you. Benjamin means "the son of God's right hand" and his original name, given to him by Rachel, was Benoni, meaning "son of sorrow." Isaiah 53:3 tells us that Jesus was a man of sorrows and acquainted with grief.

MINISTRY OF RECONCILIATION

Remember the crossing of the hands in Genesis 48? Joseph brought two of his sons to be blessed by Jacob, but the firstborn blessing ended up going to the younger son. It's like you were led in front of the Father and, even though you were not due to receive the firstborn blessing, Jesus took your sin anyway and God called you His righteousness! We understand that there was a covenant exchange made because He (God) made Him (Jesus) to be sin for us who knew no sin so that we could be made the righteousness of God. (2 Corinthians 5:21)

That sonship means that you get the double portion, which in turn means you will be a priest and a king. 1 Peter 2:9 says that you are a royal priesthood. Revelation 1:5–6 says that you are a priest and a king unto your God.

So, you have the kingship, the double portion, and the priesthood. I love the priesthood part, because it means we get to go before God on behalf of man and back to man on behalf of God—that's what a priest does. 2 Corinthians 5:18 says that we've been given the ministry of reconciliation. Just like God came to reconcile the world back to Himself, now you and I are His agents.

Ephesians 5:1 says we are to follow Jesus. When you read this scripture in the Greek, the word used for "follow" is where we get the word "mimic." So when God, through the Apostle Paul, instructed us to mimic Jesus, He was saying that we should go and do exactly what He did. Even if we don't know how to do it, God's ability will move through us to make it happen.

You need to step out in faith. You can't just wait until it feels right or until you think the conditions are right. The Bible says that those who regard the weather won't sow, so you need to step out every day and say, "I'm an agent for God. I am an ambassador of heaven." Philippians 3:20 says we are not even from here; our citizenship is in heaven. Indeed, we are ambassadors from another world.

Therefore if any man be in Christ, he is a new creature: old things are passed away; behold, all things are become new. (2 Corinthians 5:17)

We used to be just human beings, but not anymore, not since God the Father, God the Son, and God the Holy Ghost came to live on the inside of us. Jesus was divine-human and we are human-divine.

[Jesus] thought it not robbery to be equal with God: but made himself of no reputation, and took upon him the form of a servant, and was made in the likeness of men: and being found in fashion of a man, he humbled himself, and became obedient unto death, even death of the cross. (Philippians 2:6–8)

He became a man and any miracle He performed was not of Himself; God did it through Him as He yielded to the Spirit of God. Acts 10:38 says,

God anointed Jesus of Nazareth with the Holy Ghost and with power: who went about doing good, and healing all that were oppressed of the devil; for God was with him. (emphasis mine)

The operative word here is *with*. Jesus was limited in that He couldn't heal one person on His own. He didn't perform one miracle until the Spirit of God descended on Him like a dove. Then a voice from heaven said, *"This is my beloved Son, in whom I am well pleased"* (Matthew 3:17). When the Spirit of God came on Jesus in John 2, He turned water into wine by the instruction of the Spirit of God. The Bible says that this was the first of His miracles.

In Acts 1:8, He said,

But ye shall receive power, after that the Holy Ghost is come upon you: and ye shall be witnesses unto me both in Jerusalem, and in all Judea, and in Samaria, and unto the uttermost part of the earth.

This is the same power that rested on the man Jesus in Acts 10:38. He said that if you're not feeling condemned, the Spirit of God can rest upon you. When God's power rests upon you, you can get the job done.

IT'S TIME TO TAKE OVER

This is why He came, so that you would take over! We get the idea that He's coming back to take over. *"For this purpose the Son of God was manifested, that he might destroy the works of the devil"* (1 John 3:8). He said that it's our job now to enforce it. He said that the whole world is waiting for the manifestation of the sons of God in Romans 8:19, so we need to just realize who we are. The power of God has been present for more than two thousand years. This power manifested early on in the book of Acts, but there hasn't been much since.

Maybe someone will get a revelation like a John G. Lake, or maybe an Aimee Semple McPherson, or a Smith Wigglesworth. We think, *Wow, they were special!* No, they weren't any different than you; they just got a hold of the truth and began to act in authority. You need to step out and begin to act on it, begin to work it out. If you're just sitting and waiting to experience some kind of feeling, you'll never get it done.

Don't wait. It's time right now for the manifestation. It's not some future deal; it's now. You've got to stand up and take your authority. You cannot operate in the authority until you understand that it's *by grace* and *through faith* that you are forgiven.

My prayer is, "God I want to use my faith for this one thing—to be changed into Your image and into Your likeness, so that when people look at me they won't see me anymore; I'll just vanish, and the only thing left will be Jesus."

We can do this. We have the power to do all things through Christ which strengthens us (Philippians 4:13). You can be Jesus in your own house. You don't have to wait to go out on the street; you can just be Jesus at home, Jesus in your neighbourhood, praying for your neighbours instead of criticizing them.

FROM THE TRIBE OF BENJAMIN

As we look at Genesis 41 again, I want you to remember that Paul, who studied under Gamileo in the finest school in Jerusalem, would have had an intimate knowledge of everything written about Joseph and his brothers in the Old Testament. So, when he was in jail in Acts 16 and the guards beat him and whipped him, when he began to praise the

Lord at midnight, he was expecting deliverance, expecting to be taken up out of that mess. When he was told that he was free to go, he wasn't in a hurry. He wasn't hasty because he knew his position of authority.

Hebrews 3:4 talks about Moses being faithful over his house, his responsibility; then it says that Jesus was faithful over His own house, whose house are we if we hold fast until the end. We saw that Pharaoh told Joseph,

> *Thou shalt be over my house, and according unto thy word shall all my people be ruled: only in the throne will I be greater than thou.* (Genesis 41:40)

You need to see this, because this is yours now. He is the King of Kings, but you are a king. He spoke this to Joseph, but we understand the exchange of hands in all this, and Jesus turned His authority over to you.

> *And I will give unto thee the keys of the kingdom of heaven: and whatsoever thou shall bind on earth shall be bound in heaven: and whatsoever thou shalt loose on earth shall be loosed in heaven.* (Matthew 16:19)

People have a hard time with this, which is why nothing much has happened.

> *Thou shalt be over my house, and according unto thy word shall all my people be ruled: only in the throne will I be greater than thou. And Pharaoh said unto Joseph, See, I have set thee over all the land of Egypt. And Pharaoh took off his ring from his hand, and put it on Joseph's hand...* (Genesis 41:40–42)

Remember the ring from the story of the prodigal son in Luke 15:22? The ring here represents family authority. The members of Pharaoh's household would buy and sell with that ring; it was their sign of authority. When the king made a decree, it was stamped with the ring. Ecclesiastes 8:4 says that as a king and a priest unto God, you make decrees and they do come to pass. You just need to see yourself with the ring God gave you. When you say something, seal it with that authority so that you don't have to fret about it anymore.

CHOSEN FOR SUCH A TIME AS THIS

Let's look at the book of Esther. Esther and Mordecai were also Benjamites, and in the course of their story a man named Haman was planning their destruction. Instead he ended up being executed on his own gallows. Mordecai quietly rescued the king by sending him a warning, and the next thing you know Mordecai is riding on a white horse through Jerusalem, all decked out in royal robes. You are also a royal priesthood and a chosen generation (1 Peter 2:9).

Esther 3 explains what the ring represents and what it will do.

And the king took his ring from his hand, and gave it unto Haman the son of Hammedatha the Agagite, the Jews' enemy. And the king said unto Haman, The silver [representing redemptive power] is given to thee, the people also, to do with them as it seemeth good to thee. (Esther 3:10–11)

Here again, you see that the ring represented authority.

Now, when we read Genesis 41 and see that Pharaoh put his ring on Joseph's hand, we know that it represented authority there as well.

And Pharaoh took off his ring from his hand, and put it upon Joseph's hand, and arrayed him in vestures of fine linen, and put a gold chain about his neck; and he made him to ride in the second chariot which he had; and they cried before him, Bow the knee: and he made him ruler over all the land of Egypt. And Pharaoh said unto Joseph, I am Pharaoh, and without thee shall no man lift up his hand or foot in all the land of Egypt. And Pharaoh called Joseph's name Zaphnathpaaneah [supporter of life, saviour of the world, revealer of secrets]... (Genesis 41:42–45)

In Genesis 45, we can see our part in all of this. *"And I will give you the good of the land of Egypt, and ye shall eat the fat of the land"* (Genesis 45:18). Remember that John 10:10 says that Jesus came to give us abundant life, and in Ephesians 1:3 Paul writes that God has already blessed us with all spiritual blessings in heavenly places. This is the same thing!

> *Also regard not your stuff [in other words, look instead at what God has for you]; for the good of all the land of Egypt [of the world] is yours. And the children of Israel did so: and Joseph gave them wagons, according to the commandment of Pharaoh, and gave them provision for the way [for the journey home]. To all of them he gave each man changes of raiment; but to Benjamin he gave three hundred pieces of silver [representing redemption], and five [the number of grace] changes of raiment.* (Genesis 45:20–22)

Thirty is the price of redemption for a slave. Thirty times ten is three hundred, so this is exceedingly, abundantly, above all that you can ask or think (Ephesians 3:20). His grace is abounding towards you. You didn't just get a little trickle; there is an endless supply. We can see God's will here, that there is an abundant supply being provided for us.

> *And to his father he sent after this manner; ten asses laden with the good things of Egypt, and ten she asses laden with corn and bread and meat for his father by the way. So he sent his brethren away, and they departed: and he said unto them, See that ye fall not out by the way [don't stop, keep going]. And they went up out of Egypt, and came into the land of Canaan unto Jacob their father, and told him, saying, Joseph is yet alive, and he is governor over all the land of Egypt. And Jacob's heart fainted, for he believed them not. And they told him all the words of Joseph, which he had said unto them: and when he saw the wagons which Joseph had sent to carry him, the spirit of Jacob their father revived.* (Genesis 45:23–27)

When you tell your neighbours that Jesus is Lord, they may not pay any attention. It was the same way with Jacob. He didn't listen. In Genesis 45:27, his sons told him that Joseph was alive, risen from the dead. Jacob's heart fainted. In other words, he didn't believe them.

When you tell people about Jesus and they don't believe you, they need proof. You share a scripture with them, but remember that Jacob believed when he *saw*. He had to see something. We think faith doesn't require evidence, but in one sense it does, because even John the beloved disciple needed to see something to believe. The world needs to see the signs and the wonders.

Signs and wonders will follow the preaching of the Word of God. Paul said he didn't come to speak with enticing words but in demonstration of the Word with power (1 Corinthians 2:4). The church hasn't stepped out into power because we've been waiting for something to happen, for someone to do something. God says that we need to stop waiting; He's waiting on us.

When Jacob saw the wagons which Joseph had sent to him, it says that he was revived. Do you want revival and an awakening in your nation? The church is praying, "Oh God, pour out Your spirit. Oh God, move upon our nation." Let me tell you something: He already did! He said, "I'll move if you will." But we keep waiting for somebody else to do it. He didn't call somebody else; we are the ones receiving this revelation, so we need to be the ones to move with it.

Instead of looking at our circumstances, we need to remind ourselves that God is faithful and just to keep His promise. We need to go about His business and never mind our own. We like to tell people to mind their own business, but no, we need to go mind somebody else's business, leaving our own alone. God's taking care of our business and He wants us to take care of somebody else's for Him.

Genesis 45:27 says that the spirit of Jacob was revived. The word used here for "revive" is *chayah*, which can mean born again, revival, or an awakening. We use all these terms for the coming revival, the coming awakening. We are waiting for the Spirit of God to move, and I'm not saying that such things don't happen—there are times of refreshing, after all—but God has already equipped us, has already empowered us. He bought back the authority that Adam lost so that we can have dominion, so that we can take authority in the earth.

You need to look for someone who's sick, to look for an opportunity to pray for somebody. What if they don't get healed? Just say what Oral Roberts used to say: "It's not my job to heal them; it's just my job to pray for them." We need to embrace that attitude and go looking for someone to share Jesus with, looking for somebody to pray for. Believe God for a word of wisdom or a word of knowledge. Don't let the fear of making a mistake stop you.

One time, I brought an alcoholic with me to visit a pastor. This alcoholic had been having a lot of trouble. Well, the pastor looked at him and said, "Do you remember back in 1983, when you were sitting on the back steps and you asked God something? Well, today I'm giving you the answer." The guy began to cry, because that exact event had taken place. Those thoughts had come to the pastor as a word of knowledge and he simply spoke them out.

When praying for people, allow God to speak through you, because all creation is waiting for a manifestation of you. Somebody is waiting for you to be Jesus in his or her life. There's somebody on their way to Hell who needs a change in direction—they're waiting on you. We don't have to conjure it up and we don't have to feel the electricity of God; we just need to go pray for the sick and share the good news of God's grace.

TWO SIDES OF RIGHTEOUSNESS

chapter seven

THE GIFT OF RIGHTEOUSNESS

THERE ARE TWO SIDES OF RIGHTEOUSNESS—NOT TWO *KINDS*, BUT TWO *sides*. Two kinds of righteousness would be righteousness which comes by keeping the law and the righteousness from God which is a free gift. However, we're going to look at the two sides of the gift of righteousness that comes by keeping the faith. This is just like looking at two sides of the same coin. The gift of righteousness brings me into Christ, but the path of righteousness governs how I'm blessed while I'm here on this earth.

> *For if by one man's offence death reigned by one [one man messed up and brought death into the earth] much more they which receive abundance of grace and of the gift of righteousness shall reign in life by one, Jesus Christ.* (Romans 5:17)

This abundance of grace and of the gift of righteousness was given to everybody, but you have to receive it. It's the same thing Paul said in Romans 3, that Jesus Christ died for everyone on the planet but you have to believe and receive it in order for it to benefit you. You have to receive the abundance of grace. How will you know when you have it? You won't feel disgrace or shame anymore. The key point you need to see here is that *righteousness is a gift!*

In Romans 1:16, the Apostle Paul said, *"For I am not ashamed of the gospel of Christ: for it is the power of God unto salvation."* He tells us why it was so precious to him in the next verse—because in this Gospel, in this Good News, the righteousness of God is revealed. Notice it doesn't say that the righteousness of God is earned; it says that it is revealed. How? From faith to faith.

Paul goes on to tell us that the just must live by faith. Faith in what? Faith in the completed work of the cross or faith in His righteousness. Paul's talking about giving up all hope in your own righteousness and putting all of your faith in His righteousness. He says if you get a revelation in this, you'll reign in life by one Christ Jesus. In other words, you'll be in charge over your circumstances instead of being dominated by them. You won't be controlled by the sense realm; you'll be led by the spirit realm. That's why he later said,

> For he [God] hath made him [Jesus] to be sin for us, who knew no sin; that we might be made the righteousness of God in him. (2 Corinthians 5:21)

When I met Jesus, I hadn't done anything right. I lost my parents when I was very young, so I did anything that came to mind. When I met Jesus, He came to me and said, "I'm not offering you a changed life; I'm offering you an exchanged life. I'll take your sin. I already paid the price for it. Now you take my righteousness! Now you're the righteousness of God—not the righteousness of Gary, but the righteousness of God in Christ."

PATH OF RIGHTEOUSNESS

The gift of righteousness is one side of the coin. The other side is that I need to walk it out. There is a fruit to righteousness, so even though I'm already the righteousness of God, I need to learn how to walk it out. David said in Psalm 23 that the Lord will lead us in paths of righteousness for His name's sake. He is going to lead you in paths of righteousness because He wants to bless you! This path indicates a walking out of something that's in you. It's like Philippians 2:12 says—we are to work out our own salvation.

Everybody wants to see the gifts of the Spirit in operation, which is vital to the advancement of the kingdom. However, I don't hear a whole lot of people praying, "Lord, I pray that the fruit of the Spirit be in operation in my life. I pray that the love, joy, peace, long suffering, gentleness, goodness, meekness, faithfulness, and temperance be worked out in my life so that I can be changed from glory to glory, and I'll begin to look like You." When that happens, I'll begin to act like Him. When people see me, they won't see Gary the *first*; they'll see Gary the *second*.

Paul the Apostle spoke about that in Galatians 2:20. He said that he was living out his second existence. He said, essentially, "I'm not here as Paul the murderer; I'm here as Paul the Apostle, living a different life." Paul said himself that he had to die every day, and that there was nothing good in him, in the flesh. He wasn't debasing himself or putting himself down. He went on in Colossians 1:27 to say that he wanted to reveal the mystery that's been hidden from the ages. What is that mystery? That Christ is in me and in me is the hope of glory. He's in me, I'm the temple of the Holy Ghost, and He's living in me! I do have value, I do have worth, and I do have purpose on the earth. Again, the gift of righteousness brings me into Christ, but this path of righteousness governs how I'm blessed while I'm here.

KNOW YOUR ENEMY

The pivot point of the whole new covenant is John 10:10. Here Jesus says, *"The thief cometh not, but for to steal, and to kill, and to destroy."* God identified the enemy. Cancer, for example, is the enemy. It steals, it kills, and it destroys. Sin, Satan, and sickness are synonymous terms, and sickness is dis-ease. Jesus is the Prince of Peace and He said that the thief came to steal, to kill, and to destroy. God's MO, His *modus operandi*, is that you might have life, and that you might have it more abundantly.

He identified Satan, saying that he is the accuser of the brethren. When you're feeling accused, condemned, and no good, you know where it comes from because He has already told you. Then Jesus said He was going to send another Comforter, who would be just like Him. This Comforter was coming to guide us, not to shove us or knock us down. The Comforter was coming to guide us into all truth and to take the things of Jesus and the Word of God and give us revelation. Jesus said, "I'm for you. I'll never leave you, and I'll never fail you or forsake you. I'm not your problem." Many times we think He is, but He's not.

THE LAW HAD A PURPOSE

In the Old Testament, between the Ten Commandments and the six hundred and thirteen laws given thereafter, all of them were given to govern behaviour. They couldn't change us on the inside, but they could govern our behaviour. God gave them as a stopgap until a mediator came. Until the price for sin was paid, He had to have an avenue through which He could bless man. Galatians 3:24 says that the law was given as a schoolmaster to bring us to Christ. The law came to govern the Israelites' behaviour so that God could bless them. It came to change our behaviour, but Jesus came to change our hearts. Didn't He say, in 2 Corinthians 3:3, that He would write the commandments on the fleshly tables of our hearts? So, He came to give us a heart change.

The path of righteousness is still a behavioural issue. In order to walk in the fullness of the blessing, I need to walk in the fullness of obedience. Jesus said that if you love Him, keep His commandments (John 14:15). He also said that His commandments are not grievous (1 John 5:3). He's not asking a difficult thing of us because now we're empowered from within. It's not another New Year's resolution going out with the Christmas wrapping; it's something on the inside that's changing me on the outside as I yield the right of way to the Holy Ghost. Through it all,

I never feel condemned or disgraced, all because I understand that God is not mad at me.

Psalm 23:3 says that He restores my soul, which means one's mind, will, and emotions. He said, "I am in the restoration business. I'll restore you and lead you in paths of righteousness for My name's sake." The Book of Proverbs is the pathway to righteousness and I'm convinced that He gave us thirty-one chapters so that we could read one for every day of the month. It's God's wisdom, and in Proverbs 4:7 He said that wisdom is the principle thing. Wisdom is what you really need and He said we should get it—and with all our getting, get understanding. You need to go for it like it's silver or precious gold. In other words, if you want silver, you have to go find a silver mine and you have to dig it out. You have got to work for it and perspire over it a little bit. He said it's very vital.

Here's the thing about the Book of Proverbs. If you do it all, it won't earn you any brownie points with God, and if you don't do any of it, you won't lose your salvation. You're doing it for your own benefit, so that you can walk in the fullness of the blessing because you're the righteousness of Christ.

COVENANT KINDNESS

Isaiah 54:9 says,

For this is as the waters of Noah unto me: for as I have sworn that the waters of Noah should no more go over the earth; so have I sworn that I would not be wroth with thee, nor rebuke thee.

What He's saying to you is that there's no need to run and hide. As an immature Christian, when I messed up the last place I wanted to be was in church. I just wanted to get away. I felt ashamed because I didn't have this teaching, and I didn't receive it for a long time. Now that I have it, you can't pull it out of my hand because there's freedom and liberty in this. I now have the ability to live a holy life without struggle.

Let's take a look at Isaiah 54, which prophesies Christ's resurrection.

"For the mountains shall depart, and the hills be removed; but my kindness..." (Isaiah 54:10). One translation says "my grace." The Hebrew word is *hesed*, which means covenant kindness. Covenant kindness isn't based on anything I've done. Remember Hebrew 6:13, when God said He couldn't swear by anything greater, so He swore by Himself? He made a covenant with God the Father. He was referring to Genesis 15, when He made a covenant with Abram. The first thing He did with Abram was knock him out; a deep sleep came upon him, getting him out of the way, because sometimes he was led by his flesh. The Bible says that a burning lamp and a consuming fire passed between the sacrificial pieces, giving you the idea that God the Father made the covenant with Christ the Son.

Paul explains this in Hebrews 6 where he tells us two immutable things: God the Father cut covenant with Christ the Son, and it is impossible for God to lie. We have a strong consolation, a hope, an anchor for our souls. Because He could swear by nothing greater, He swore by Himself.

When I went to court as a young man, I had to lay my hand on a Bible and repeat after the judge, "I swear to tell the truth, the whole truth, and nothing but the truth, so help me God." Well, God did the same thing, only He would have said, "I promise to tell you the truth, the whole truth, and nothing but the truth, so help me, Me." It's impossible for Him to lie and He could swear by nothing greater, so He swore by Himself this covenant: "I'll not be wroth with you. I will not rebuke you."

Again in Isaiah 54:10 we read,

> For the mountains shall depart, and the hills be removed; but my kindness shall not depart from thee, neither shall the covenant of my peace be removed, saith the LORD that hath mercy on thee.

Who is the Prince of Peace? In order for peace to be removed, the Prince of Peace would have to be removed, and that's not going to happen.

ESTABLISHED IN RIGHTEOUSNESS

In Isaiah 54:14, it says, *"In righteousness shalt thou be established..."* You need to become established in righteousness, because in it there's no fear of penalty. You have no reason to hide. You have no reason to lie or cheat, and no reason to sin. Sin is just a feeling, like I'm lacking and have to do something to fill an empty spot. Once you fill it up with righteousness, there's no longer any emptiness. Being established in righteousness simply means that you're more aware of *His* works than your own. It's not based on what you're doing; it's based on what He has already done. Once I realize what He's done, I'm empowered to do what I need to do without fear of penalty.

Look at this promise:

In righteousness shalt thou be established: thou shalt be far from oppression; for thou shalt not fear: and from terror; for it shall not come near thee. Behold, they shall surely gather together, but not by me: whosoever shall gather together against thee shall fall for thy sake. (Isaiah 54:14–15)

You do have an enemy on this earth. If you ever think you'll get free of that, let me tell you that it will require your death. This is a war zone, which is why Paul told us in 1 Timothy 6:12 to fight the good fight of faith. Any time you start to operate in faith, you're brought into a fight. So fight and lay hold of eternal life.

Facts are real, but the outcome of the fight is determined by you. That's what He talked about in Isaiah 53:1. *"Who hath believed our report? And to whom is the arm [strength] of the LORD revealed?"* If you believe God's report instead of the doctor's report, you can walk out healthy. If you believe the doctor's report, or how you're feeling, above what the Word of God says, you will die. You'll still go to heaven, so it's not a total loss, but God said the final decision is yours. Are you going to believe God's Word or are you going to believe the circumstances? It's always a decision and you get the final choice.

There's no way to disconnect one word from another. Jesus also said in John 16:33,

These things I have spoken unto you, that in me ye might have peace. In the world [this world] ye shall have tribulation: but be of good cheer; I have overcome the world.

How can you overcome the world? Make a choice: choose to be happy. You can choose to be sad or mad, or you can choose to be happy. Tell yourself, "I'm not letting circumstances rule me. I'm not letting other people control me. God gave me self- control."

Behold, they shall surely gather together, but not by me: whosoever shall gather together against thee shall fall for thy sake. (Isaiah 54:15)

When your enemies gather together against you, they will fall. Say this, "Fall fear, fall terror, fall oppression, in Jesus' name."

Behold, I have created the smith that bloweth the coals in the fire, and that bringeth forth an instrument for his work; and I have created the waster to destroy. (Isaiah 54:16)

In other words, He made the smith that brings forth the instruments of destruction. He created him, and you can handle him.

When you see people being deceived, you ask yourself how that could possibly happen. Then you realize that Satan, right in front of God Almighty, deceived one-third of the angels into following him and rebelling against God. Satan is obviously capable of seduction, and you need to know the Word and be established in it. Peter said it this way, and I paraphrase, "I'm telling you things that you already know, but I'm telling it to you fresh so that you can be established in this present truth" (2 Peter 1:12). It's not what you *knew*, it's what you *know*! Faith comes by hearing, not by having heard. Faith comes by hearing and hearing by the Word of God, so you need to be established in this present truth.

No weapon that is formed against thee shall prosper; and every tongue that shall rise against thee in judgment thou shalt condemn.

This is the heritage [your blood-bought right in Christ] of the servants of the LORD, and their righteousness is of me, saith the LORD. (Isaiah 54:17)

So, your righteousness comes from Him! You didn't earn it; you received it by faith, and therefore you keep it by faith. When you keep it by faith, James 5:16 says that the effective, fervent prayer of a righteous man avails much. That's you, because it's not your righteousness—it's His. Once you realize it's His, you can pray powerful prayers, because it's not based on your performance. His desire for you is to be a champion and to live victoriously.

The word "condemn" appears there in verse seventeen. What this means is that people who come against you will be proven wrong by the way it turns out. Sometimes it will happen next week and sometimes it will happen in five years. If you hang with God and don't seek your own vengeance, leaving it all to God, you can watch and see what He does. I've watched it happen time and time again.

ONE MEDIATOR

Let's look at Job's dilemma with trying to find righteousness. Job had some troubles, most of which we know he brought on himself. In Job 3:25, he said, *"The thing which I greatly feared is come upon me."* Fear will bring things into your life just like faith will, but fear brings the things that you don't want. Job was in a dilemma: *"I was not in safety, neither had I rest, neither was I quiet; yet trouble came"* (Job 3:26). Yet we see the first chapter of Job begins with him being an outwardly righteous man. Outwardly he looked good, but his righteousness was all about performance; he couldn't be the righteousness of Christ like you and I are.

In Job 9, he sees his dilemma:

If I wash myself with snow water, and make my hands never so clean; yet shalt thou plunge me in the ditch, and mine own clothes shall abhor me. For he is not a man, as I am, that I should answer him, and we should come together in judgment [come together and discuss things]. Neither is there any daysman betwixt us, that might lay his hand upon us both. (Job 9:30–33)

In the margin of my Bible, it says "umpire" for the word daysman. Job was saying that he needed a mediator, somebody to intercede on his behalf, someone to represent him before the throne of God—but he couldn't do it because he was a sinful man. He recognized his problem.

In Ezekiel 22, we're going to find out that God had the same problem. You mean God had a problem? Yeah, He had a problem—and He solved it. You were created and put on this earth to solve problems, and you're created in the image and likeness of God. You were born to be an overcomer. How can you overcome if there's not something to overcome? How can you fight the good fight of faith if there's no opposition? How can you walk by faith and not by sight if everything you see looks good? You've got to have some problems. Problems are good. Paul the Apostle said it this way in 2 Corinthians 4:17: *"For our light affliction, which is but for a moment, worketh for us a far more exceeding and eternal weight of glory."* In other words, these light afflictions are working for us. They're nothing compared to the glory that will be revealed in us. He realized that the things coming against him were resistance training; he was getting stronger and his enemy was getting weaker. He was learning how to depend on God and how to be strong in the Lord and not strong in his own way, like he used to be when he was a murderer.

In Ezekiel 22:30, God was looking for a man just like Job was in Job 9:33. He was looking for a man to be his mediator.

And I sought for a man among them, that should make up the hedge, and stand in the gap before me for the land, that I should not destroy it: but I found none.

Sin requires judgment. Without the shedding of blood, Hebrews 9–10 both say that there is no remission for sin. God needed a man and Job needed a man. We understand that God had a plan in place; Jesus was slain before the foundation of the world. He wanted you redeemed as much as you wanted redemption, and even more so. God was looking for a man and Abraham was as close as He could come. At least Abraham was willing to offer up his son and gave God the right to offer up His in covenant relationship.

According to 1 Timothy 2:4, all men need to be saved. That's the number one priority. Number two is for people to come into the knowledge of the truth. What is number three? That's discipleship. You can run around and get people saved, but God said all you're creating is a spiritual Calcutta by abandoning the young ones and not taking time to disciple them. You need to take time to disciple people and get them into the Word of God, because it's the entrance of His Word that brings light. If you don't give people the Word of God, you're not giving them anything. You need to give them the Word while being established in the Word of God yourself.

> *For there is one God, and one mediator between God and men, the man Christ Jesus; who gave himself a ransom for all, to be testified in due time.* (1 Timothy 2:5–6)

There's only one mediator between God and man, Christ Jesus, and He came to pay the price for sin once and for all. Once was enough. It wasn't the Son of God, but Jesus the man. He shed His blood so that you could be free, shed His blood so that Job could come out of the place where he was incarcerated—a place called "Abraham's Bosom," also known as Hades. I encourage you to read Hebrews 9–10, circling "once" and "one" every time you see them.

Romans 9:29–32 says,

> *Except the Lord of Sabaoth [the Lord of Host, the Lord of armies] had left us a seed, we had been as Sodoma, and been made like unto Gomorrha. What shall we say then? That the Gentiles, which followed not after righteousness, have attained to righteousness, even the righteousness which is of faith. But Israel, which followed after the law of righteousness, hath not attained to the law of righteousness. Wherefore?*

This is because righteousness comes by faith, and they couldn't keep the Ten Commandments.

Think about how strict those commandments were. Jesus said, "If you look at a woman and lust after her, you've already committed adultery in your heart" (Matthew 5:28, paraphrased). What He was basically saying was that if you just think about sin, you're guilty by the law. Why was that? God used the law as a schoolmaster to bring you to Christ. It's impossible to keep every law. You can't do it! That's what He was waiting for. He was waiting for you to throw up your hands and say, "I can't do this."

I have a pastor friend who said, "That's it, God, I quit!" and God said, "Good, now we can get something done. Now that you're out of the way, I can work with you." The principle here is that unless the Lord builds the house, they who labour, labour in vain. Unless the Lord builds anything, they who labour, labour in vain. Unless the Lord builds your business, unless the Lord builds your marriage, unless the Lord builds your finances, you labour in vain (Psalm 127). It's just a vain thing.

So nobody could keep the law, as we see in Romans 9:32.

Because they sought it not by faith, but as it were by the works of the law. For they stumbled at that stumblingstone.

It's like me wanting a new Mercedes Benz, but I'm going to try building my own. That means I have to mine and process the iron. Then I have to get a machine shop and buy some machinery. Then I have to make the engine, then get a paint job. Then I've got to do the fenders… and on and on. It's going to take me a while, if I could even get it done in a lifetime, right? But why would I do that when I can go to the Benz dealership and buy one that's already been built? That's how futile the law is. You're trying to build it yourself, but it's already been built in Jesus. So if you accept what He's done, you can stop building and start enjoying the drive! You'll never enjoy the drive as long as you're trying to build it yourself.

So they stumbled at it, but Romans 9:33 says,

As it is written, Behold, I lay in Sion a stumblingstone and rock of offence [Jesus]: and whosoever believeth on him shall not be ashamed.

If you're ever feeling shame, it's because you don't believe what He did. Conviction comes from the Holy Spirit while condemnation comes from the devil. He said that whoever believes on Him has righteousness. Remember, when Paul ended Romans 9, the topic was righteousness. He said that when you believe on Him and believe by faith, you will not be ashamed. You'll take the word "disgrace" and scratch the "dis" right off it, leaving it as grace. You'll be free—not free to sin, but free to serve Him with a pure heart.

Isaiah had a revelation of this. He said,

I will greatly rejoice in the LORD, my soul shall be joyful in my God; for he hath clothed me with the garments of salvation, he hath covered me with the robe of righteousness... (Isaiah 61:10)

He couldn't do anything to help himself. He was looking to the future at the cross, whereas we're looking back at the cross, but the cross was the only way then, and it's the only way now.

SEATED FAR ABOVE

Ephesians 1:19 says,

And what is the exceeding greatness of his power to us-ward who believe, according to the working of his mighty power.

Paul uses four different Greek words for power in this passage: *energia, ischys, dynamis,* and *kratos.* Paul wanted you to understand this revelation so bad that he pulled out every word he could think of to convey to you how powerful it is.

And what is the exceeding greatness of his power to us-ward who believe, according to the working of his mighty power, [the same power] which he wrought in Christ, when he raised him from the dead, and set him at his own right hand in the heavenly places. (Ephesians 1:19–20)

Get out your Bible and circle the word *Him.* Then draw a line down to Ephesians 2:1, where it says *And you.* This is talking about one event, not two separate events. When God raised Jesus up, He raised you up—and it wasn't a parallel experience. It wasn't Him *and* you, it was Him *and you in Him,* a single experience when He set Him in the heavenlies. You can say that He did the same thing with you because, if you look at Ephesians 2:1, it starts with *"And you…"* See, the head needs the body to carry out the plan. So, God's head is in heaven and He wants His will done on the earth. He wants to see people saved, delivered, set free, and filled with the Holy Spirit, but it isn't going to happen until the body cooperates.

Let's say that I'd like to have a drink of water. My head could want that all day long, but if my body doesn't cooperate I could die of thirst. So, now my head wants a drink of water and I don't even have to think about it; my body is programmed to obey. I just reach my hand out and get a glass, fill it with water, and take a drink of it. God wants to program you to obey.

Let's go back and personalize Ephesians 1:21—"And *you* who were dead in trespasses and sins, *you* were raised up far above all principality and power and might and dominion" (Ephesians 1:21, paraphrased). How do I know that? Because I'm His body. If you look in Ephesians 1, you'll see that the body went when the head went—and I'm His body. It's Christ in me, the hope of glory (Colossians 1:27).

Jesus said it this way in John 15:

I am the vine, ye are the branches: he that abideth in me, and I in him, the same bringeth forth much fruit: for without me ye can do nothing. If a man abide not in me, he is cast forth as a branch, and is withered; and men gather them, and cast them into the fire, and they are burned. If ye abide in me, and my words abide in you, ye shall ask what ye will, and it shall be done unto you. (John 15:5–7)

Why? Because I'm hooked up, I'm in the flow. What's flowing in the head is flowing through the body. You can't separate me from God; I'm hooked up to Him. I can separate myself, but I don't want to. If you want out, it's because you've never been in. *"O taste and see that the LORD is good"* (Psalm 34:8). Once you've tasted Him, nothing else tastes good.

It's like the woman at the well. She had five husbands and was living common law trying to fill that empty space. There wasn't a man on earth who could do it until the man Jesus came and sat at the well and said, "I've got some water for you. If you'll drink it, you'll never thirst again."

"Oh Lord, how are You going to get it?" she asked. "You don't have anything to draw the water from."

He said, "You don't know what I'm talking about. I'm talking about *mayim hayim*—living water."

There's a water you can drink. There's a presence of God in your life that, once you taste it, the things of the world will grow dim.

JESUS DIDN'T DIE IN VAIN

Ephesians 2:3–7 says,

Among whom also we all had our conversation in times past in the lusts of our flesh, fulfilling the desires of the flesh and of the mind; and were by nature the children of wrath, even as others. But God, who is rich in mercy [not cheap in mercy], for his great love wherewith he loved us, even when we were dead in sins [even on your worst day, Christ died for you], hath quickened us together with Christ, (by grace you are saved;) and hath raised us up together, and made us sit together in heavenly places in Christ Jesus: *that in the ages to come he might shew the exceeding riches of his grace in his kindness toward us through Jesus Christ.* (emphasis mine)

When I got a revelation of this, it changed my prayer life. Now I'm not praying *to* heaven, I'm praying *from* heaven. That one simple thing

111

changed everything, because now I'm in a position of authority—and not my own authority, not my own righteousness. I'm in a place of authority because He sat me there in Him. Revelation 1:5 says that you are priests and kings unto God. 1 Peter 2:9 says that you are *a royal priesthood... [to] shew forth the praises of him who hath called you out of darkness into his marvellous light.*

And the work of [the action or path of] righteousness shall be peace; and the effect of righteousness [will bring me] quietness and assurance for ever. (Isaiah 32:17)

Therefore, I'm not struggling by trying to be something. I'm not a Christian *doing*; I'm a Christian *being*. I'm already there. I am complete in Him who's the head of all principality and power, and now I realize that my walk is all about governing my own behaviour. The teaching in the Word of God is there so I can walk in the fullness of the blessing. That's what I'm doing.

1 Corinthians 15:34 says, *"Awake to righteousness, and sin not..."* In other words, once I recognize that I am the righteousness of God in Christ, and I'm not struggling and trying to *be* that, I'm accepting it as a done deal. Then I can live it out and walk in righteousness.

In Psalm 66:18, David said, *"If I regard iniquity in my heart, the Lord will not hear me."* Notice he didn't say, "If *God* regards iniquity in my heart, He won't hear me." He said, "If *I* regard iniquity in my heart, the Lord will not hear me." Why? I can't pray in faith when I'm feeling guilty and I can't pray for anybody when I'm feeling ashamed. I can't be a good witness for Jesus when I'm feeling like a rat myself. Most people never bring people to the Lord because they don't feel like they're worthy. Well, if you're not worthy, Jesus died in vain.

He died to make you worthy! You can be bold like Proverbs 28:1, which says that the righteous, those who understand His righteousness, are as bold as lions. If you're timid and fearful and ashamed, you haven't figured out that you're righteous yet. Once you know you're righteous, the spirit of faith will make you bold. It's like a tadpole slapping a whale; it'll do something on the inside of you to make you feel bigger than your surroundings. It doesn't matter how big your circumstances are. It doesn't matter how big your enemy is. The stronghold over a city, the strong man over a city, has got to come down. How? You just keep hitting him with the Word of God. How long does it take? Well, God promised your victory. He said that if you fight the good fight of faith, you'll win, but He didn't promise you a first round knockout. He promised you a victory.

A COMPLETE EXCHANGE

chapter eight

IT'S NOT JUST A MAKEOVER

GOD MADE A COVENANT WITH JESUS AND THIS COVENANT BROUGHT each one of us into right relationship with God. The whole Bible is about two men—the first Adam and the second Adam. The first Adam, the natural man, only became a natural man when he fell from his place of grace. The second Adam was a life-giving spirit, Jesus Christ. When Adam committed high treason against God, he brought something into the earth called sin—or sickness. Sin, sickness, and Satan all mean the same thing and Jesus came to undo them. When Adam committed high treason against God, he felt disgrace and shame and he ran and hid. Jesus came to bring grace for that disgrace. He came to restore man to his rightful place!

Hebrews 2:10 says that the captain of our salvation is made perfect through suffering the temptations you are tested with. He was made perfect through that and came to restore many sons back to glory. God is in the restoration business, and it's not just a makeover—it's a brand new building!

> *Therefore if any man be in Christ, he is a new creature: old things are passed away; behold, all things are become new.* (2 Corinthians 5:17)

TWO SIDES

In order for anything to be balanced, it has to have two sides. Take anointing, for example. There is the front side of anointing and a back side. The backside of the anointing will wipe you out. That doesn't mean you go to hell, because once you've received the gift of righteousness your destination is heaven. You may just get there sooner than you planned. We could call this "the two sides of grace" or "the two sides of faith."

If you deface one side of a coin, it becomes valueless. Lots of times we preach one side of something too much and neglect the other side. My wife Nancy and I determined earlier this year that we would teach both sides of the Gospel, so that we would all understand that one side of grace (or righteousness) is our relationship with God and the other side is our relationship with others.

Grace is not a divine permission for us to live wrong and get away with it; grace is a divine impartation to do what's right to reign in life. Grace is God's answer to man's sin. It's God's mercy that delivers us out of trouble and His grace that keeps us from sin. Grace requires no obligation on behalf of the one on which it is bestowed. Grace is the word that expresses the difference between one's futile attempts to win God's favour and the way in which a personal relationship with God is actually developed. It's not working to be accepted, it's allowing His love to envelop you now because God opposes the proud but bestows grace to the humble. Works are not the cause of salvation, but the result—an expression of how I feel toward God.

ABUNDANCE OF GRACE

For if by one man's offence [Adam's] death reigned by one; much more they which receive abundance of grace and of the gift of righteousness shall reign in life by one, Jesus Christ. (Romans 5:17)

What God did in Christ is greater than what Satan did in Adam. It is much greater! It is overshadowed by the abundance of grace. It's like being born again; Jesus died for the whole world, but it only works for those who receive it (Romans 4:24).

Romans 5:17 says that we who receive the abundance of grace and the gift of righteousness shall reign in life by one Christ Jesus. Paul means that once you understand that you have a right relationship with God, you will be put in a place of kingship and authority. To reign means to dominate, and to reign over something gives you dominating power; it gives you influence and it gives you royal authority. We see this in Ecclesiastes 8:4—*"Where the word of a king is, there is power."*

Revelation 1:5–6 tells us that we are priests and kings unto God. 1 Peter 2:9 says,

But ye are a chosen generation, a royal *priesthood, a peculiar people; that ye shew forth the praises of him who hath called you out of the darkness into his marvellous light.* (emphasis mine)

In Ephesians 2:6, we see that God has given us a position in Him: *"[Christ] hath raised us up together, and made us sit together in heavenly places in Christ Jesus."* You are seated in heavenly places with Christ. You have been given this place of authority, but you must believe it and you must receive this abundance of His grace.

JUSTIFIED BY FAITH

How do you receive something? If I were going to give something to my friend, all he would have to do is reach out and take it from me. He wouldn't need to earn it, because I'm offering it to him. God is offering you His righteousness. He (God) made Him (Jesus) to be sin for us who

117

knew no sin, that we might be made the righteousness of God in Christ (2 Corinthians 5:21). He is offering us *right standing* with Him.

Romans 5:1 says that you are justified by faith and have right standing with God your Father through your Lord Jesus Christ. He came to make you right even when you're wrong. You couldn't do enough right to make yourself right; that would be self-righteousness. He came that we might receive this abundance of grace and the gift of righteousness and begin to reign over sickness, to reign over sin, to reign over darkness, to reign over poverty, and to reign over depression, or whatever else is coming your way. Just because that's the way it is doesn't mean that's the way it stays.

I AM WHAT I AM

In 1 Corinthians 15, Paul talks about this gift of righteousness, and then about the work of righteousness—or, as David said in Psalm 23:3, *"He leadeth me in the paths of righteousness for his name's sake."* Your path is not who you are; your path is where you're going. Where I'm walking doesn't define who I am; it's simply where I'm going. The gift of righteousness brings me into favour with God and the path of righteousness brings me favour on the earth, governing how I am blessed while I'm here.

1 Corinthians 15:10 says, *"But by the grace of God I am what I am."* Paul wasn't making excuses. I've heard this passage used that way, too: "It's just the grace of God that I am what I am." In other words, he's saying that he doesn't have to change, but that's not it. We live an exchanged life, not a changed life. We are being changed from glory to glory as we yield to the Holy Spirit. There's supposed to be change in our lives. If I am the same way now that I was five years ago, then I haven't been doing anything different. I've just been doing the same thing. God said, "No, you need to change." How many of you know that even a baby's diaper smells better after it's been changed?

> But by the grace of God I am what I am: and his grace which was bestowed upon me was not in vain; but I laboured more abundantly... (1 Corinthians 15:10)

118

Paul established first of all that it was God's grace that was *given* to him. He couldn't earn it. After he received that grace, he began to work. Religion will have you working for it, but grace will have you working as a result of it. I could do everything the Word of God says and not earn anything more. Because I have received the gift of righteousness, I can do everything in the Bible. I could preach eight days a week and I could fast. I could do anything and not have a more right position with God than I have right now. It wouldn't change my position in Him. Now, if He leads me to do those things, then I will do them, but I'm not doing them to try to earn something from Him. I'm doing them because it's a response to how much I love Him. My motivation always needs to be love.

Paul said that he laboured more abundantly than all of the apostles, but then he goes on to say, *"Yet not I, but the grace of God which was with me"* (1 Corinthians 15:10). There was no air in his head; he was just a humble man. He said that whatever happened was because of God.

Psalm 23:1 says, *"The Lord is my shepherd…"* That means I have somebody guiding me. I'm not doing my own thing. I am *being* led, I'm not leading. The Lord is my shepherd, and as a result I shall not want. He makes me to lie down in green pastures. He wants me to live an abundant life. I know some people are opposed to prosperity, but Paul says in 3 John 2 that he wishes above all else that we should prosper—that you will prosper, that you will be in health even as your soul prospers. God leads me beside the still waters and restores my soul—my mind, my will, and my emotions. He restores me and reminds me that He loves me. He builds me up. He encourages me and He leads me. I don't lead myself; He leads me.

How many of you have led yourself into a mess and then God somehow took that mess, after you repented, and turned it into a message? Nonetheless, you could have looked back and said, "God, why did you let me do that? I can't believe you let me do that. You know everything." His answer would have been, "I tried to talk to you, but you were strong in yourself. Don't worry. I love you enough to bail you out. I know your heart is right even when your head is wrong."

"He restoreth my soul: he leadeth me in the paths of righteousness for his name's sake" (Psalm 23:3). Again I want to remind you that the *gift* of

119

righteousness brings you into Christ and the *pathway* of righteousness governs your behaviour while you're here.

RESISTANCE TRAINING

In the New Testament, the Christians had a heart change, while in the Old Testament all God could do was change the Israelites' behaviour, so He gave them the Ten Commandments. He didn't give the Ten Commandments because He wanted to be mean; He gave them because He needed the people to know, "The better you act, the more I can bless you." Just like natural children, when your kids are doing things right, you want to help them. When they are wrong, you still want to help them, but you know you can't because you can't bless bad behaviour; if you do, the bad behaviour never changes. For some reason, we think God is different than natural parents, but He's not. He came to change my heart so that I could live a victorious life. I understand now that my relationship with God doesn't change, but my relationship with others will change as I behave properly towards them.

The Ten Commandments came with the law, but grace didn't. Thank God we're not under the Ten Commandments; we have a higher standard to live by now. We must walk out the law of love, and when we do we're not going to break any of those Commandments anyway. Can you even recite them? So many people claim that we're supposed to live by the Ten Commandments, but I haven't met anyone yet who could actually quote them all. Thank God most people can quote Psalm 23, because that's what we need to be led by.

If you allow the fruit of the spirit in Galatians 5:22—love, joy, peace, longsuffering, gentleness, goodness, faithfulness, meekness, and temperance—to be worked out in your life, you'll have a happy life. Does that mean people won't still bother you and things won't come against you? If you're in a fight right now, I want to encourage you. Your struggles aren't going to stop until Jesus takes you home, but I've found that I get stronger as I keep fighting.

We are just like David. His faith developed so much through his years of adversity. Adversity is good for you! I know nobody likes it, but when you fall into diverse temptation, tests, and trials, have yourself a party. Why? Because somehow it's as though 2 Corinthians 4:17 is working for you:

> For our light affliction, which is but for a moment, worketh for us a far more exceeding and eternal weight of glory.

I know that afflictions are against you, but they also work for you, making you stronger—just like weight resistance training at a gym. It's hard to move that weight, but after a while, after practice, it becomes easier.

DON'T RUN AND HIDE

Isaiah 53 depicts the death, burial, and resurrection of the Lord Jesus Christ. Isaiah 54 follows that by letting us know what's going to happen after the death, burial, and resurrection of the Lord.

> For this is [like] the waters of Noah unto me: for as I have sworn [made you a promise] that the waters of Noah should no more go over the earth; so have I sworn that I would not be wroth [angry] with thee, nor rebuke thee. (Isaiah 54:9)

In other words, when Adam sinned, he ran and hid. But God says, "You don't need to run and hide when you mess up. You need to come to Me so we can work this through. Come to Me, your loving Father. You have right standing with Me."

Hebrews 4:16 says, "Let us therefore come boldly unto the throne room of grace." And not just when we've got it all together, but to obtain mercy and to find grace in our times of need. You can skid into home plate and say, "Help, Jesus. Look what I just did. Can You fix it? Will You forgive me?" His reply will always be, "Yes, son, I'll fix it and, yes, I forgive you."

I want to share with you the Hebrew version of this portion of Scripture in Isaiah 54:

> For the mountains may leave and the hills be removed, but my grace will never leave you, and my covenant of peace will not be

121

removed," says ADONAI, who has compassion on you. Storm-ravaged city, unconsoled, I will set your stones in the finest way, lay your foundations with sapphires, make your windows shine with rubies, your gates with garnet, your walls with gemstones. All your children will be taught by ADONAI; your children will have great peace. In righteousness you will be established. (Isaiah 54:10–14, CJB)

Notice that last verse: *"In righteousness you will be established."* That right there is the key to this whole passage of Scripture.

Once you're established in this truth, you can walk it out. That doesn't mean that your circumstances won't be bad; it means that your circumstances will have to change because you are established in the fact that you're right with God. If God is for you, who can be against you? God is on your side, you will not be afraid. It gives you the backbone you need to live in these last days and perilous times.

In righteousness you will be established, [you will be] far from oppression, with nothing to fear; far from ruin, for it will not come near you. Any alliance that forms against you will not be my doing; whoever tries to form such an alliance [against you] will fall because of you. It is I who created the craftsman who blows the coals and forges weapons suited to their purpose; I also created the destroyer to work havoc. No weapon made will prevail against you. In court you will refute every accusation. The servants of ADONAI inherit all of this; the reward for their righteousness is from me. (Isaiah 54:14–17, CJB)

This is good. People need to know this. All my life, I've heard Christians say, "God, why did You let this happen? God did this to me to try to teach me something. I'm sick because God's trying to teach me something." If that was true, then Christians ought to be the smartest people on earth—but instead we still haven't learned anything. It's a lie, a religious lie. God said,

The thief cometh not, but to steal, and to kill, and to destroy: I come that they might have life, and that they might have it more abundantly. (John 10:10)

God is not your problem. He is your answer.

In other words, the thief is a created being; he's not all-powerful like you and me, who have been created in the likeness and image of God. He is a created being—and you are in right relationship with God. You are in a safe place.

He that dwelleth in the secret place of the most High shall abide under the shadow of the Almighty. I will say of the LORD, He is my refuge and my fortress: my God, in him will I trust. (Psalm 91:1–2)

The devil isn't going to come around you when you're walking with God. God has His arm around your shoulder and you are in a safe place. There are all kinds of circumstances going on, but He said, "I came that you might live above the fray." Don't get caught up in it. Don't live down in the natural realm.

No weapon made will prevail against you. In court you will refute every accusation. The servants of ADONAI inherit all this; the reward for their righteousness is from me. (Isaiah 54:17, CJB)

The righteousness that came from Him produces the reward. Let's read it in the King James Version.

No weapon that is formed against thee shall prosper; and every tongue that shall rise against thee in judgment thou shalt condemn. This is the heritage of the servants of the LORD, and their righteousness is of me, saith the LORD. (Isaiah 54:17)

Now, that's pretty plain!

A FREE GIFT—NOT OF WORKS

I believe God has laid these things on my heart because in my travels, over the past couple of years in particular, I have seen that the best message anybody could ever preach is the message of grace. Everybody needs it. You need to understand that you have value and worth. The message of grace has been perverted to the point where people think it means you can just live any way you want to, just go off by yourself and do whatever you want because God loves you no matter what. That's not true. Well, it's only part of the truth, but it's not the whole truth. I do whatever *He* wants me to do because He loves me. That is the true message of the Word of God.

In Ephesians 2:8–10, we see a good illustration of both sides of righteousness.

> *For by grace are ye saved through faith; and that not of yourselves: it is the gift of God: not of works, lest any man should boast. For we are his workmanship, created in Christ Jesus unto good works, which God hath before ordained that we should walk in them.*

We are saved by grace, through faith. It's a gift of God. We access grace through faith, not by our works. Faith can only work on what grace has already provided. This gift of God, which we saw earlier in Romans 5:17, is the gift of righteousness.

Ephesians 2:9 says that this gift is not of works, lest any man should boast. That's one side of the coin. The next verse says that we are His workmanship, created in Christ Jesus unto good works. So, we see here that righteousness is the gift of God and that it's not of works. You cannot earn it, but the good works are a *result* of our right standing with God. In other words, the path of righteousness is the works that He's talking about in Ephesians 2:10.

I cannot substitute one for the other. I cannot go to God and say, "Lord, I'm believing You for such-and-such because I preach and I'm reading the Bible all the way through again this year, and I'm doing lots of holy things and I treat my wife right." That's coming to Him based on what I'm doing, instead of what He's already done. Those works are something that I could boast about, but we see in Ephesians that it's not about works.

When I receive His gift of righteousness, I can't go to Nancy and tell her off, then walk away and say, "I'm the righteousness of God in Christ." I can't do that anymore than I can go to God and say, "Look, I'm doing all this good stuff." I can't go to God with my good works, and I can't go to Nancy with, "I am the righteousness of God," and still act goofy or be disrespectful. The *path* of righteousness—the works of righteousness or my righteousness—is my relationship or my behaviour toward you. The *gift* of righteousness is my dealing with God.

In 1 Timothy, it gets a little plainer:

For bodily exercise profiteth little: but godliness is profitable unto all things, having promise of the life that now is, and of that which is to come. (1 Timothy 4:8)

That would be the paths of righteousness, or the works of righteousness, which is to come. The two sides of the gift of righteousness are the blessings that I experience in this life and that which is to come. This gift of righteousness is the only way by which I can get to heaven. I cannot get to heaven based on my own merits. It won't work to say, "I've done this and I've done that." This is what Paul talked about in Romans 10:3, that the Jews were ignorant of God's gift of righteousness, so they went about trying to establish their own righteousness. You can never do enough right things to make you right with God. It's simple: by faith you receive, access His grace, and become the righteousness of God.

The *gift of righteousness* is the only way to heaven, but the *works of righteousness* is the only way I will receive honour on this earth.

I can pray, "God, I thank You that I'm increasing in favour with You and with man," but the only way that I'll increase in favour with man is if I treat others with respect.

So many times, Christians spend all their time praying about themselves. Really, if I'm going to fulfill the law of love, I ought to spend more time praying for you than I'm praying for me. I'm not condemning you if that's the way you've been, but we need to grow from that state.

We need to make other people our priority. I find that the more time I spend praying for others, the less I'm wrapped up in my own concerns. God somehow just takes care of those concerns.

DEPART FROM INIQUITY

In 2 Timothy 2:19–21, we can see how walking out righteousness brings us to a place of honour. It won't increase our salvation and it won't make us any more right with God. We have already been born into His family.

I know a Christian who is sitting in jail right now. He was backslidden, but as far as I know he's still the righteousness of God in Christ. If the church was called home today, there would be an empty jail cell, unless he totally denounced the family of God, like Esau did, and said, "I don't want anything to do with that."

How many of you have children who didn't do everything right while growing up? Did you ever disown them? Even if you may have felt like you should, of course you didn't. They're part of you. It doesn't matter what they've done, you would die for them. God is just like that.

Nevertheless the foundation of God standeth sure, having this seal, the Lord knoweth them that are his. And, Let every one that nameth the name of Christ depart from iniquity. (2 Timothy 2:19)

To depart from means to turn away and go in another direction. There is nothing mysterious about it. Isaiah 53:10 says that it pleased the Lord to bruise Jesus. If you want to know how God feels about sin, watch Mel Gibson's *Passion of the Christ*. Even that won't describe it, because in religious circles we've taught that Jesus received thirty-nine stripes, but that was a Jewish law. The Romans beat Jesus, and Isaiah 52:14 says that He was marred beyond man, or beyond recognition. The Good News Bible says that "he hardly looked human." He was rubble hanging on the cross and there was no flesh left.

The sin question is settled, but He hasn't changed His attitude toward sin. He loves the sinner, but He still hates sin. He hates it so much because it is destructive. He didn't say, "Thou shall not commit adultery so that you won't have any fun." He gave that command because He knows adultery will rip you apart, your kids will suffer, and this pain will then be carried into the next generation. The consequences of sin are horrendous; that's why He told us not to sin. It's like the highway sign on the off-ramp that says "Wrong Way." That sign isn't there because someone didn't want you taking a shortcut; if people took that shortcut, they could end up being hit by an eighteen-wheeler!

> *Let every one that nameth the name of Christ depart from iniquity. But in a great house [God's house] there are not only vessels of gold and of silver, but also of wood and of earth; and some to [have] honour, and some to [have] dishonour.* (2 Timothy 2:19–20)

I'm glad He didn't stop with that verse, because you would always be trying to figure out if you qualify. In the next verse, He tells us how to qualify.

> *If a man therefore purge himself from these, he shall be a vessel unto honour, sanctified, and meet for the master's use, and prepared unto every good work.* (2 Timothy 2:21)

He wants to use us, but He needs our minds to be renewed. That's why He gave us these scriptures:

> *I beseech you therefore, brethren, by the mercies of God, that ye* present your bodies a living sacrifice *[just like He submitted His dead one], holy, acceptable unto God, which is your reasonable service. And be not conformed to this world: but be ye transformed by the renewing of your mind, that ye may prove what is that good, and acceptable, and perfect, will of God.* (Romans 12:1–2)

THE POWER TO LIVE RIGHT

I believe that Romans 12:9 is going to help you to understand and it's not going to make you religious. That's the danger when you preach the other side. All of a sudden, people get so wrapped up in having to do everything right that they get all stiff. You need to remember that it's not about your performance; it's about this knowledge, because knowing the truth will set you free.

You and I have the power within us to live right. If I get in an argument with my wife, I know how to go back to her and say, "Please forgive me." It's as easy as pie. I've done it often. You know humble pie? I like it now. It tastes pretty good to me, like lemon meringue. It's the same with God. If I mess up, I say, "God, please forgive me. I don't want to do anything to bring shame to Your name. I'm not trying to earn brownie points with You, I just want to be a good representative. I just want people to see You."

Romans 12:9 says, *"Let love be without dissimulation. Abhor that which is evil; cleave to that which is good."* God set a standard for what is evil and what is good, but we live in a society where the devil cannot create anything; nonetheless, he works to reprogram you. Both God and the devil want to reprogram you, but the devil does it subtly over time. When *Three's Company* first came on the air, back in the 1970s, people were shocked by it. It was about two girls and a guy living together in one apartment. The thought that people would live together without being married, and especially two women and one guy, was just scandalous. However, just look at what's on television now! As Christians, we're supposed to abhor that which is evil, but we now just accept a lot of these things because we don't want to be religious about it, or we don't want to act super holy. If evil things are seeping into our lives, it's like a little bit of arsenic at a time—it's not doing you any good. So, if it's not doing you any good, just turn it off. We need to make sure grace doesn't lower the bar; it raises the bar so that we are to live at a higher level.

You can't hide behind the works of righteousness in your dealings with God. That means I can't say, "Lord, look at everything nice I did for you." Because it's not based on what I'm doing; it's based on what He did. I can't hide behind the gift of righteousness in my relationship with you.

Psalm 2 tells us the Lord sits in the heavens and laughs (Psalm 2:4). Zephaniah 3 says that He rejoices over us with singing (Zephaniah 3:17). We should be the happiest people on the planet, shouldn't we?

After all, we're on our way to heaven. We have it made in the shade! I don't know how big your mansion is in heaven, how many acres it sits on, but I think you'll like it.

BEWARE OF THE FRUIT

Matthew 7:15 tells us to beware of false prophets, those who come to you in sheep's clothing, but inwardly they are ravenous wolves. That means they look like sheep—they have on sheep wool, sheep ears, and sheep noses, but they're not really sheep. God said that you'll know who they really are by their fruit. Matthew 7 begins by telling us not to judge others, but as you read further we find out what we *are* to judge.

Ye shall know them by their fruits. Do men gather grapes of [from] thorns, or figs of [from] thistles? Even so every good tree bringeth forth good fruit; but a corrupt tree bringeth forth evil fruit. A good tree cannot bring forth evil fruit, neither can a corrupt tree bring forth good fruit. Every tree that bringeth not forth good fruit is hewn down, and cast into the fire. Wherefore by their fruits ye shall know them. (Matthew 7:16–20)

I'm allowed to look at you. I'm allowed to look and see the fruit of your life. I cannot judge your relationship with God, but I can look at the way you treat others to see either the works or the walk of righteousness. God tells me that this is how I should judge others. I am to judge the path of righteousness that they're walking. This is the only thing I'm allowed to judge. I'm not allowed to judge your relationship with God.

Paul, when he was writing the book of 1 Corinthians, said,

But with me it is a very small thing that I should be judged of you, or of man's judgment: yea, I judge not mine own self. For I know nothing by myself; yet am I not hereby justified: but he that judgeth me is the Lord. Therefore judge nothing before the time, until the Lord come, who both will bring to light the hidden things of darkness, and will make manifest the counsels of the hearts: and then shall every man have praise of God. (1 Corinthians 4:3–5)

129

Paul is saying, "I don't even care that you're judging me. I don't know whether you're saying I'm not qualified to be a pastor. I don't even judge myself. It's not good to judge anything before its time." He's talking about relationships, not the walk of righteousness.

We read in Matthew 7:20 that you will know who people really are by the fruit of their lives. That would be one side of righteousness, but then the next verses say,

Not every one that saith unto me, Lord, Lord shall enter into the kingdom of heaven; but he that doeth the will of my Father which is in heaven. Many will say to me in that day, Lord, Lord, have we not prophesied in thy name? and in thy name have cast out devils? and in thy name done many wonderful works? And then will I profess unto them, I never knew you: depart from me, ye that work iniquity. (Matthew 7:21–23)

This is how God judges. He doesn't judge people's works; He judges their relationship with Him. They come to Him trying to be righteous by what they've done, but they haven't received the gift of righteousness. Therefore He says, "Depart from Me. I don't even know who you are."

Without receiving the gift of righteousness, you don't have a relationship with God and you aren't part of His family. It doesn't matter how many good works you do. I'm talking about people who are out there trying to do good works and trying to earn their way to heaven. If nothing changes, they will be sadly disappointed. They'll have worked so hard and it's all in vain.

What a tragedy it is to work so hard at living a good life and then hear God say, "Depart from Me. I don't even know who you are." That is tragic! That's why we need to live the good life in front of those who are still trying to earn it. You and I have a freedom that they don't have, a freedom which they can't have because they're still trying to earn their right with God whereas ours came for free. We received it for nothing!

the struggle is over

As I CLOSE OUT THIS BOOK, I WANT TO REMIND YOU ONCE AGAIN THAT you cannot lose the *gift* of righteousness unless you flat out throw it away. That gift is your position in God. Remember, the *gift* of righteousness brings us into Christ, but the *path* of righteousness governs our behaviour in life.

In Psalm 23:3, we see that God leads us in paths of righteousness for His name's sake. This path is not who you are; it's simply where you're going. You already are the righteousness of God in Christ according to 2 Corinthians 5:21, which says,

> *For he [God] hath made him [Jesus] to be sin for us, who knew no sin; that we might be made the righteousness of God in him.*

We have righteousness with God our Father and nothing can separate us from that. Now we are learning to walk in that path of righteousness.

The book of Proverbs teaches us wisdom to walk in the paths of righteousness. The righteousness of God in Christ is my heavenly connection and the paths of righteousness exist so that I can walk out my salvation. We understand the Old Testament came to govern our behaviour and the New Testament came to change our heart. God began teaching this in Jeremiah 31. He wanted Jeremiah to tell the people that in the last day He was going to write His commandments upon their hearts. He was going to walk with them and they would walk with Him. He would be their God and they would be His people. (Jeremiah 31:33) God wanted them to know that it wouldn't be an exterior thing anymore. Religion is still trying to change us from the outside, but we are being changed from the inside and the greatest changes come when we get a revelation of how much God loves us. After that, everything else will fall into place.

In the Old Testament, we understand that God couldn't change man's heart, but He worked on their behaviour so that He could bless them. The better their behaviour, the more He could do for them. Now He's written His laws in our hearts and wants us to know that He has given us the power and grace to walk in this path of righteousness. The earthly blessing still comes as a result of us walking out our righteousness and working out our salvation. That's why we see that some people are more blessed than others. Are they more righteousness than anybody else? No, we're all the same when it comes to being in Christ and being righteous. If we stay on the path of righteousness, we will be safe. It's only when we get off the path that troubles come.

As a child, I remember my friends and me climbing a fifty-foot cliff on our way to school. There was a path alongside of it which our parents would really encourage us to use. We didn't use it, though, because it was more of an adventure to go up and down the side of the cliff. However, if we had fallen, whose fault would it have been?

If you get off the path, a snake can bite you. When you get off the path, you may get lost. There is a path of righteousness and Proverbs really is that path. This path of righteousness doesn't earn us any brownie points with God, but it enables Him to be a bigger blessing in our lives. Just like a parent with a child, parents are better able to bless their children when they're doing everything right. We don't love our children any less when they mess up, but it limits what we can do for them without wrecking their lives. God is no different.

Get a revelation that He's not mad at you. He's not upset about anything you've done. God's not out of joint because of something you did last week, last month, or last year. Receive what the psalmist said about Him in Psalm 23:3—*"He guides me in paths of righteousness for His name's sake."* He said He would lead us, so just let Him lead. When you let Him lead, you're not trying to change things from the outside, struggling to be just good enough.

David wrote many of the Psalms as he received revelation from God about walking in the path of righteousness. The Bible says that Jesus increased in wisdom and stature, and favour with God and favour with man (Luke 5:52). He had favour with man because he was walking out what he was getting from God. I can tell everyone I'm a Christian, but until I begin to demonstrate it to the world, nothing much changes. Churches will fill up when they see us living successfully. It won't be a problem witnessing to people. Our life will be a witness. People will see that we have something that is attractive to them. We don't seem to be troubled in perilous times. We aren't wringing our hands in worry. There's something so peaceful about our lives and it comes with knowing that we're loved.

The reason most Christians don't demonstrate this is because we're really not sure if God loves us or not, because we don't think very highly of ourselves. We're disappointed with ourselves. God would ask you, "How can you be disappointed with yourself?" The day that you were born again, you became more successful than billions of other people on this planet. The greatest, most successful thing you will ever do happens the day you bow your knee and say, "Jesus, I can't do this on my own, but I'm so glad that you already did it." Now just yield to Him and live victoriously in this life!

a p e r s o n a l   d e c l a r a t i o n

I AM THE RIGHTEOUSNESS OF GOD IN CHRIST. THAT IS MY TRUE IDENTITY and I will not keep it a secret.

I am what the Bible says I am, I have what the Bible says I have, and I can do what the Bible says I can do. Therefore, I declare right now that because Jesus has already paid the price for my shame and guilt, I am released from condemnation. I'm free from guilt and shame and I live in the fullness of God's grace.

I am the blood-bought, Holy-Ghost-taught, spirit-filled, tongue-talking, devil-chasing child of the Most High God. As His child, I walk free from condemnation. I am free from guilt and shame. I'm not inferior and I refuse to believe Satan's lies.

I see myself seated in Christ and filled with His love. I see myself as He sees me, through the blood of His dear Son. His grace has removed my shame just like His blood has completely annihilated my sin and

He sees it no more. Therefore, I refuse to look at my past, and where I messed up, to determine my self-worth or determine my future. I see my future in Jesus, through His blood and through His grace.

Thank you, Lord, that today I am free from the guilt of my past. Thank you, Lord, that I am the righteousness of God in Christ Jesus and nothing I do can make me any more righteous than I am right now.

I allow Jesus to dwell in me fully, causing me to overcome in every area of my life. According to Paul's prayer in Ephesians 3, I declare that Christ dwells in my heart by faith and that I'm rooted and grounded in love. I know the love of Christ, which passes knowledge, and I am filled with all the fullness of God.

God's Word is all the education I will ever need to be victorious in this life! I don't accept condemnation when I miss it, so the enemy has nothing to use against me. Colossians 2:20 says that I'm already complete in Him, and nothing I do will make me any better than complete!

a b o u t   t h e   a u t h o r

GARY WAS ONLY SIX YEARS OLD WHEN HIS FATHER DIED. WITH HIS mom passing away shortly after his tenth birthday, he was uprooted from his home and thrown into an unfamiliar environment. Feeling abandoned, unwanted and alone led him into a life of lawlessness and rebellion. At age 15, he and two friends slammed a stolen car into a concrete wall. Gary was the lone survivor. Alcohol and drugs were the fuel that took him through many encounters with the police, a failed marriage and a series of jobs. He stood at the graveside of several close friends who had their lives snuffed out because of drug addiction and related problems.

Motorcycles and intoxication are a dangerous combination. This lifestyle brought with it four trips to the hospital, where he waited several months for his body to heal or several days for the drugs to wear off, then back to the party. Landing in a Drug Dependency Centre for the second time, Gary accepted Jesus as his Lord and Saviour when a member of the Gideons came and shared the love of God with him.

His hunger for the Word of God and his compassion for people inspired him to start a church. In 1992, Gary along with his wife Nancy founded New Covenant Ministries in the living room of their home and stepped out into full time ministry in 1994. Then in 1998, the church purchased a 15,000 square foot building, which now houses a congregation numbering over 250 people - to the glory of God!

Since 2003, Gary has been reaching homes across North America through a weekly television broadcast, KnightLife TV, aired on the Miracle Channel & WJHJ-TV.

Gary is an anointed preacher and teacher of the integrity of God's Word and justification by faith. New Covenant Ministries is a family oriented church that has something for everyone. Together, Pastors Gary and Nancy welcome you to join with them in leading the body of Christ from tradition to truth.

To contact Gary Hooper, please write, email or call:

PO Box 28063 Dartmouth, NS B2W 6E2

Email: gary@newcovenantchurch.ca

Phone: (902) 468-(WORD) 9673